OF MOOSE AND MEN

TORRY MARTIN & DOUG PETERSON

HARVEST HOUSE PUBLISHERS
EUGENE, OREGON

Unless otherwise indicated, all Scripture quotations are taken from the Holy Bible, New International Version®, NIV®. Copyright © 1973, 1978, 1984, 2011 by Biblica, Inc.® Used by permission. All rights reserved worldwide.

Verses marked KJV are from the King James Version of the Bible.

Cover by Harvest House Publishers, Inc.

Front and back cover photos of author © Rory White, rorywhite.com

Cover photos © Amorphis, GreenApple78, Avalon_Studio, Rawpixel Ltd / iStock

OF MOOSE AND MEN

Published by Harvest House Publishers
Eugene, Oregon 97402
www.harvesthousepublishers.com

Library of Congress Cataloging-in-Publication Data
Martin, Torry
Of moose and men / Torry Martin and Doug Peterson.
pages cm
ISBN 978-0-7369-6526-2 (pbk.)
ISBN 978-0-7369-6527-9 (eBook)
1. Martin, Torry, 1961- 2. Christian biography—Alaska—Biography. I. Title.
BR1725.M264A3 2016
277.3'083092—dc23
[B]

2015016853

Printed in the United States of America

16 17 18 19 20 21 22 23 24 / VP-JC / 10 9 8 7 6 5 4 3 2 1

From Torry
To Robert Browning,
the Abbott to my Costello, the Lewis to my Clark,
and sometimes the Lex Luthor to my Superman.
But most importantly, the David to my Jonathan.

From Doug
To Dave and Leanne Lucas,
traveling companions and "milepost friends" for Nancy and me.

ACKNOWLEDGMENTS

I must begin by thanking my best friend, Robert Browning, because without him I would have probably been mauled by a grizzly bear, stomped on by a moose, or been killed in just about any other way you can imagine in the Alaskan wilds. But what he did for me was so much more than that. Rob also saved me from myself. He supported me in my writing, investing in me and encouraging me every step of the way. As far as I am concerned, friends don't get any better than Rob.

I would also like to thank those who helped me to survive spiritually in the wilderness—my "milepost people." In addition to Rob, these include Pastor Jack and Ann Aiken, whose church became a wilderness outpost of love and encouragement; Dean and Larry Lauer, whose lives blazed a spiritual trail; and Kay Arthur, whose Precept Ministries Bible study materials became my spiritual survival kit. (When I was living in our Alaskan cabin, going through Kay Arthur's Bible studies, I never dreamed that one day she and her husband would invite me to their house and cook me a chicken dinner. Life takes some surprising turns!)

Meanwhile, those who have helped me to survive along the writing trail include my regular writing partner, Marshal Younger of *Adventures in Odyssey*, and Doug Peterson, my coauthor on this book.

Finally, I want to acknowledge my parents, Billy and Verna Martin, whose sense of humor has made life a true adventure, and who bring the joy of Christmas into every season of the year.

I struck gold with friends and family like this.

CONTENTS

PREFACE

Rob slammed on the brakes, bringing our truck to a squealing, skidding stop. I was asleep in the passenger seat, but the screech startled me awake, and I looked up to see a beautiful, 40-plus-pound lynx standing stock-still in the middle of this Alaskan road, staring back at us.

Having never seen a lynx before, I knew it was an opportunity to get a once-in-a-lifetime photograph, so I quickly threw open the door and leaped out, camera in hand. I was just moving beyond the open door when I heard Rob bellow from behind the steering wheel of our Chevy Silverado.

"Torry! Get back in here! NOW!"

His sudden shout startled the lynx, and the animal dashed into the woods, disappearing just like that. As far as I was concerned, Rob had just ruined the photograph of a lifetime.

"What's the problem?" I asked. "I could have had his picture in another second."

"He could have had *you* in another second!" Rob shot back.

"He was smiling."

"He was *growling*!"

"Fine, a loud purr," I compromised. "The point is, Alaskan lynx are probably used to tourists. I'll bet he was trained to stop for photo ops. Until you went and scared him off. Poor kitty."

Rob sighed. He did that a lot around me.

This brief incident as we entered Alaska was prophetic in many ways because I would go on to have many more wildlife encounters on the Last Frontier. Unfortunately I wouldn't always have Rob there to keep me from doing incredibly stupid and dangerous things. Keep reading and you will see exactly what I mean.

We drove from Silverdale, Washington, to Anchorage, Alaska, in May of 1993. I was leaving behind my life as an actor in Los Angeles, and Rob was hoping to stake a mining claim in Alaska. So we made the grueling 2284-mile, 40-hour journey, following twisting roads and carrying all of our life's possessions behind us in a trailer. For much of the trip, we traveled the famous Alaska-Canadian Highway—the Alcan Highway, which begins in Dawson Creek, British Columbia, and winds its way up to Delta Junction, Alaska.

Rob handled much of the driving while I did the navigating by using my hefty volume of the legendary Alaska travel planner, *The Milepost*. Everyone who has any sense brings along *The Milepost* when they travel the Alcan Highway. This guidebook tells you exactly what you will encounter, mile after mile, on the way to the Last Frontier. It tells you what you will see, where to stay, where to eat, where to find gas, and on and on.

I just wish everything in life could be spelled out for us so clearly.

I am pretty sure that when the Israelites made their way to the Promised Land, the Lord didn't give them a *Milepost* travel book that told them exactly what they could expect as they wandered through the wilderness. Besides, they wandered in circles for 40 years, so they would have been bored out of their minds reading the same *Milepost* information over and over and over. What I'm trying to say is that it's the same with our lives. The Bible is chock-full of guidance, but God doesn't spell everything out for us. Life is a holy adventure, and it is for us to discover, milepost after milepost.

As you will soon see, our life in Alaska was not easy. We lived day by day, barely having enough to live on and nearly freezing to death in a cold camper in the middle of nowhere. From a materialistic viewpoint, I had virtually nothing. But today, looking back on those years, I realize that I had so much spiritually. In fact, after revisiting these stories—the mileposts in my life—I see that this was perhaps my happiest time.

My years in Alaska weren't easy, but that's the point. Sometimes the hardest years are the happiest because they force us to put our trust in God. I call it Desperate Christianity, and my years in Alaska were desperate but glorious.

When the Israelites reached the Promised Land, one of the first things Joshua had them do was pile up a stack of rocks in honor of God. Each rock was a memory, a remembrance of what God had done for them along the way. People today still build these stacks of rough rocks—"cairns" they call them.

The stories in *Of Moose and Men* make up my "cairn," my way of remembering what God did for me in the wilderness of Alaska. Each story is a stone in my stack, a tribute to a time that God worked a wonder in my life.

These stories are also snapshots of my own mileposts—the times when God kept me on the road as I swerved crazily from side to side, trying to avoid the potholes of sin. Sometimes, I'm sorry to say, I found myself purposely aiming for one of these gaping potholes and getting a jolt of reality when I soon got stuck.

Life is not easy, and I have to make a daily choice to follow God. Even then, I still mess up, and there are days when I get lost in a blizzard of my own foolish choices and God has to lead me back to the road. If you take the time to look back at the milestones in your life, you might be surprised at the number of times that God was at work, bringing you out of the blizzard and into His warmth.

So bundle up in your long underwear and grab your bunny boots because we have just crossed the Canadian border and entered Alaska.

Milepost number one is coming into view.

Torry (right) and Rob. In the Alaskan wilderness, it's best if you've got a buddy who will watch your back. It's even better if it's someone you can outrun. (Rob has me on that one.)

Cabin Vertigo. Also known as "Incinolet Sweet Incinolet." Read on. You'll find out what I'm talking about.

1 THE PRODIGAL REINDEER

The 400-pound reindeer was going berserk, desperately trying to get out of my kitchen. Wild-eyed, it bashed me against counters and appliances as it tried to turn around in my tiny kitchen, its feet slipping and sliding on the slick floor and its black hooves clicking on the plywood like tap shoes.

Now freeze-frame the scene: That's me there. I'm the one without the stubby antlers—the bearded, extra-large, hippie-looking human with blazing red hair flying in every direction, mouth wide open in terror. I look like a frightened Bigfoot in overalls.

So how did I find myself in this predicament? How did I wind up with a full-grown reindeer in my kitchen? It started when I first opened my eyes on this cold, cold morning. It always seemed to be cold in Bear Valley, just southeast of Anchorage, Alaska. And on mornings like this, I could think of nothing better to do than hibernate.

Bears can hibernate because they don't have a phone by their bed to disturb them, but I wasn't quite so lucky. The ring of the phone slapped me out of my slumber, and I clumsily put the receiver up to my ear and growled something that was clearly unintelligible. You probably would have gotten a more lucid response from an actual bear.

My best friend and co-cabin-dweller, Rob (Robert Browning—no relation to the poet), was on the other end of the line telling me something about a reindeer, but I was lost in the fog of sleep. He said something about looking outside the window, but all I remember saying was, "Yeah, yeah, I'll be sure to do that just as soon as I wake up. Right now my pillow is missing me." Then I hung up the phone, closed my eyes, and got back to the serious business of hibernating.

A half hour later: the phone. It was Rob again.

"Did you take care of the reindeer?" he asked.

"That's Santa's job," I said, getting ready to hang up again.

But this time he wasn't going to be so easily dismissed. Rob's voice rose a hundred decibels or more. "Get out of bed and look out the window NOW!" Then he slammed down the phone with such force that I'm surprised the sound from the receiver didn't dislodge the snow on the roof.

That woke me up. I crawled out of bed and stumbled to the window. There I saw a rather large reindeer wearing a bridle. It was standing just a few feet from the window and calmly staring back at me. It was a peeping reindeer! I quickly pulled on my pants just in case he had a camera.

This time, it was my turn to make the phone call. "Rob," I said, "there's a reindeer outside our window."

I could hear an audible groan of exasperation.

I learned that Rob had discovered the reindeer on his way down to the main road earlier that morning. We lived in an odd little L-shaped cabin on 80 acres of Alaskan wilderness, and he had come across the reindeer on his way to his truck. The animal wore a bridle and collar, so it obviously belonged to someone. Rob had patiently walked the reindeer all the way back to our cabin and tied it to a tree using a tow strap from his truck. Then he took off for work, figuring he would call me on his way and have me take care of it.

"What am I supposed to do with a reindeer? Buy a sleigh?" I asked Rob. "How do you even know it's safe? That thing is the size of a pony!"

"Stop freaking out. He's tame," Rob said, probably repeating what he had already told me before on the phone when I was half asleep. "There's a collar on him with a tag and a phone number. Go get the number and call the owner."

Rob also suggested that I dig out some carrots and other vegetables from the refrigerator to feed the reindeer. So I did as I was told and went back outside. Never did I imagine, in all my years of living in Los Angeles, that I would be standing in snowdrifts in the middle of a forest feeding carrots to an Alaskan reindeer.

Rob was right. The reindeer was friendly. Almost puppylike. But I didn't have a pen and paper to write down the number from the reindeer's collar, so I headed back into the cabin. Then came my crucial mistake. I decided to bring the reindeer into the cabin to save myself a trip back outside and to share the indoor warmth with this large creature. I figured he must be as cold as me.

Sometimes it's worth taking an extra trip.

The front door of the cabin led directly into our tiny kitchen; and when I opened the door, the reindeer happily marched inside as if I had just opened the barn door. But I hadn't thought through what I was doing. If I had taken any time to really think, I would have remembered one important wildcard: Sam.

Sam was our dog—and not a small one either. Sam was part Labrador, part Airedale, and all Big.

Up to this point of the story, Sam had been lounging on the sofa in the living room, watching out the window and thinking typical dog thoughts, which were probably more advanced than my thoughts on this frosty morning. I'm sure he was wondering why I was leading this strange animal through the front door of his personal kingdom. Sam did not charge us rent to live in his domain, but if he had given us a lease to sign, it would definitely have said, ABSOLUTELY NO REINDEER IN THE CABIN!

The moment the reindeer clomped into the kitchen, Sam came charging in our direction, barking and snarling like a dog possessed. The reindeer panicked. Not a good thing to happen in such a small kitchen. To give you an idea of just how small our kitchen was, I could put my foot on the wall on one side and reach out and touch the wall on the opposite side. The kitchen had not been designed to hold a 130-pound dog, a several-hundred-pound reindeer, and a human who weighed approximately...well, let's not go there. You get the idea.

Sam was not going to let the reindeer get any farther into the house, and the poor creature must have thought I had intentionally led him into this trap. So the reindeer did what any animal would do when trapped in a tiny kitchen. He went nuts. He decided he had to get back outside immediately, and he didn't care who stood in his way—which would be me.

My kitchen became a pinball machine, and I was the pinball. The reindeer's muscular body slammed me into the wall. Ouch. Then he sent me hurtling against our metal cabinets. Another ouch. Then I felt the impact of the kitchen counter against my side. I could almost hear the "ding, ding, ding" of the pinball machine as I caromed from one side of the kitchen to the other. Then I hit the refrigerator.

On top of the refrigerator sat a huge plastic container in which we stored approximately 50 pounds of flour, purchased in bulk from Costco. I was sent hurtling against the refrigerator with such force that this container of flour came cascading down like an Alaskan avalanche of snow. Covered in flour, I turned as white as a ghost, and so did the reindeer and Sam. I stumbled through the cloud of flour, trying to blink it out of my eyes and still getting bashed by the out-of-control reindeer. Sam, whose jet-black fur was now as white as a bedsheet, was still barking and snarling at the poor reindeer. At some point, I stubbed my toe against the foot of Dasher or Dancer or Prancer. Whatever this guy was called, the point was that our feet connected, and it was painful.

All covered in flour, I must have looked like a crazed version of the Pillsbury Doughboy—the Abominable Doughboy. But somehow, some way, I managed to get the front door open. I opened it just enough to let the rampaging reindeer escape. Then I slammed the door closed—WHAM!—keeping Sam inside the cabin, where he continued to bark wildly. With my heart still racing, I found myself back outside and back in the cold as I turned to face the reindeer. He had already calmed down considerably and was just standing there staring at me, as if to say, "Okay, big boy, how about some more carrots?"

At that moment, it hit me. I hadn't needed to worry about how cold this animal felt—Comet or Cupid or Donner or whatever his name might be. He's a reindeer! He has *two* layers of fur and is built for the cold. How could I have been so stupid? So I retied the reindeer to the tree and retrieved the pen and paper without bringing this claustrophobic animal along.

When I finally had the phone number from the reindeer's collar, I dialed it immediately, and the person answered, "Brewster's Department Store."

Brewster's Department Store? What was this reindeer doing with the phone number for Brewster's, one of the oldest, most revered establishments in Anchorage? Was he a frequent shopper? And what am I supposed to say to them? "Hello, I've got a reindeer I'd like to return, but I don't have a receipt."

Instead, I told the woman that my name was Torry Martin and that I lived in Bear Valley. I wanted to make it clear to this woman that I was a normal Alaskan, if such a thing existed, so she wouldn't think I was crazy when I said my next sentence. "I have a reindeer at my house, and he has the department store number on his collar."

"A reindeer?" the woman said, completely baffled.

"Yes, with a collar with your number."

"Oh, really?" she said. I could tell the woman wasn't buying it. Then I heard her shout to someone in the background. "This guy's got a reindeer at his house with a collar and our telephone number!"

The person in the background went nuts. "It's Rudy! It's Rudy!" She yanked the phone out of the other person's clutches and said, "You have Rudy?"

"Who's Rudy?" I asked.

"Rudolph!" the woman exclaimed. "He's Mr. Brewster's reindeer!"

Rudolph the reindeer. Of course. (I would have gotten to that name eventually.)

The name Brewster was also quite familiar. Charles H. Brewster was an Anchorage icon. He was the famed founder of Brewster's Department Store and an inductee into the Alaska Business Hall of Fame. You could usually find this gentle soul in his department store wearing a cowboy hat and cowboy boots, and he was famous for his line of winter clothing. Every Fourth of July, he dressed in silver and rode in the Anchorage parade on his palomino horse, Honcho.

But Charles Brewster was best known for his classic commercials, which always featured a young and energetic person talking a mile a minute about all of the store's great deals. Then the camera switched over to the elderly Mr. Brewster, who stared straight at the camera and said in his creaky voice, "And if I'm in the store, I'll wait on you myself."

I must have seen these commercials a million times. And every time I saw this elderly, slow-moving, slow-talking man tell viewers he'll wait on them himself, I would think, *Who's got that kind of time? Glaciers move faster.*

The woman on the other end of the phone told me that Mr. Brewster was working a full shift today. Would I mind keeping an eye on Rudy until five o'clock? I told her, "Sure, but I'm babysitting a moose at six, so make sure he doesn't dawdle."

Only in Alaska.

So along comes five o'clock, and Mr. Brewster calls me on his cell phone, telling me he's having a hard time finding my place. I told him to look for the big sign that says, "Danger! Warning! 4-Wheel Drive Only! Chains Required! Enter at Your Own Risk!" That reassuring sign means you're about to turn onto the road to our cabin.

As I led Rudy down the trail leading to the road, I fully expected Mr. Brewster to be waiting there with a horse trailer or at least a pickup truck. So you can imagine my shock when I saw Mr. Brewster drive up in what appeared to be a Cadillac—a long, fancy car. Anything that isn't a broken-down Jeep looks like a Cadillac to me.

I'll never forget what happened next. Good old Mr. Brewster got out of his car, dressed in his trademark cowboy hat, boots, and red-and-black checkered flannel coat. He walked right up to Rudy and wrapped him in a big bear hug.

"Rudy!" he shouted gleefully. "Where you been, you little bugger?" Mr. Brewster was talking to Rudy as if he were one of his children—a long-lost son.

Then it dawned on me. Rudy was the prodigal reindeer. Rudy once was lost, but now he's found. He was dead, but now he lives.

In case you haven't flipped through Luke 15 of the Bible recently, it records the story of a son who had the audacity to demand his share of his father's inheritance. In that culture, asking for the inheritance before your father passed away was tantamount to telling him you wished he were dead. So, with money jangling in his pockets, the prodigal son hit the open road, settled in a distant country, and spent the money on every possible pleasure, which if it had been me would have been cupcakes and comic books. But he didn't count on the famine that soon hit the land, leaving him penniless and dying of hunger.

Rudy the reindeer had also been looking for freedom when he broke away from his master. For the first hour or two, he probably was having a grand time, bounding around on the outskirts of Anchorage. But by the time Rob came across him, he was hungry and scrounging for food on a snow-covered landscape and most likely wondering why he had ever left his master's side.

Like the son in the Bible story and like the reindeer, I too have led a prodigal life. I too had run from my Master, squandering my inheritance on raucous living. I had run away from God, but in Alaska I found that He hadn't run away from me. On the Last Frontier, God tracked me down.

Which leads me to the end of this story of the reindeer...

After hugging Rudy, Mr. Brewster turned his attention to me, standing there in my Carhartt overalls—the warmest, most durable clothes made. Carhartts are among the most popular clothes in Alaska, and I wore a pair 90 percent of the time.

"I tell you what," said Mr. Brewster, sizing me up. "You come in the store and I'll give you a couple pairs of those Carhartts as a thank-you."

I was thrilled. And as Mr. Brewster handed me Rudy's leash, he said, "Just a minute." He climbed inside the car, and I'm looking into the backseat and thinking, *How in the world is this guy going to fit a reindeer in the backseat of a Cadillac? And since when do reindeer have chauffeurs? I thought it was usually the other way around.*

When Mr. Brewster was finally settled in the driver's seat, he rolled down the window and asked me to hand him the leash. So I did.

"All right, Rudy, let's go," he said.

Then Mr. Brewster tipped his cowboy hat and began to drive away. Slowly, he turned the car around and started down the road, holding onto Rudy's leash and leading him alongside the car. "Stop by and pick up your overalls!" he shouted as I watched the car inch its way down the road. "And if I'm in the store, I'll wait on you myself!"

In the parable of the prodigal son, the father welcomed his wandering son home with open arms, sprinting from a long distance just to greet him. In Jewish culture back then, a noble man always walked because that was a sign of dignity. But the prodigal's father didn't care—he ran to his son as fast as his old legs would carry him. Let people think him a fool; he had a son to welcome home.

In our culture, driving your car slowly, as Mr. Brewster was doing, would be viewed as similarly foolish. American cars are all about speed, but like the prodigal's father, Mr. Brewster didn't care. He had a reindeer to welcome home, so he drove away going only about seven or eight miles an hour with Rudy alongside.

As Mr. Brewster drove off with Rudy trotting happily by the side of his car and the sun just beginning to settle on the Alaskan horizon, I felt as if I were watching an old Western movie. I understood then that I was not just watching a foolish prodigal reindeer return to the safety and love of a kind, gentle master. I was watching my life.

God led me back to Him in the same gentle way Mr. Brewster led Rudy back home. God didn't drag me back, kicking and screaming. He didn't force His love on me. He also didn't pull me along faster than I was prepared to go. He took it slow. He had the patience that only a loving God could display.

I believe that God tries to speak to us every single day through the events that happen to us, even when they're not as dramatic as a reindeer in your kitchen. When I was living in Alaska, I had fun looking back on each day and trying to find the spiritual significance in it. What else did I have to do with my time in a desolate, snow-covered cabin?

This book is all about the stories I lived and the lessons I learned. These are the parables of my life.

We are all prodigals finding our way back to God. We are all lost souls looking for our way home. *Of Moose and Men* is the story of how I found my way back to God in Alaska, the Last Frontier. It's the story of how the Ruler of the universe gave me a big bear hug, looked me in the eyes, and said, "Where you been, you little bugger?" And it's the story of how God will redeem, reclaim, and repurpose all of us for His perfect will.

After all, God is always in the store, and He'll even wait on us Himself.

2
SHAKE, RATTLE, AND ROAR

I don't mind caviar on a cracker, but fish guts on a picnic table in the Bird Creek Campground? Not on my watch. I had already told this guy he needed to clean his fish down by the water, not in the camp, but clearly he had ignored me.

The man's RV carried New York license plates, which meant he was probably better suited to tracking down a Starbucks in the city than deer bucks in the wild. His idea of essential camping gear was a state-of-the-art espresso maker, and roughing it would be equipping his RV with a 20-inch television rather than a 42-inch screen. This guy really knew how to put the recreation in "recreational vehicle." Nevertheless, he still saw himself as a cross between Crocodile Dundee and Daniel Boone, so he wasn't about to listen to me.

"Dude, I already told you once—you need to clean your fish down by the water," I said, folding my arms across my chest. "Bears. You'll attract bears."

"I ain't gonna attract no bears, so fuhgeddaboudit." His mafioso tone told me not to mess with him or I might find myself sleeping with the fishes—or at least sleeping with the fish guts. I was a camp host, which meant I carried a little less authority than a mall cop.

Rob and I were newcomers to Alaska when we stumbled across this job as floating camp hosts, moving from state park to state park, giving breaks to the regular camp hosts whenever they needed a vacation. Our task was to check in campers, keep the peace, and remind people not to do stupid things to attract bears and other wildlife into the camp. It was kind of like babysitting except we couldn't give the campers a time-out, as much as I tried.

And believe me, I knew something about babysitting. One of my first jobs in Alaska had been on Anchorage television as a local Fox Kids Club host, introducing Disney cartoons and doing special events for hordes of wild children. It took me four long months to discover I wasn't cut out for kids. They were dirty, loud, and easily distracted. In short, we were far too similar to get along.

In addition to being an expert on kids, I had flung my fair share of fish guts. One of my other early jobs in Alaska was at a caviar factory, scooping eggs out of the bellies of fish with my hands—a salty, stinking job that ate away at my skin. Two weeks was all I could stand there. The camp host job was a breeze in comparison except when it came to dealing with petulant campers.

Which brings me back to the New Yorker at Bird Creek…

As if the fishy remains on the guy's table weren't enough to lure all the local wildlife, the man left hamburger buns out at his campsite. He might as well be walking around in a sandwich board that said, "Attention All Bears! Free Food! Everything Must Go!"

Everybody in Alaska knew that if a bear stopped by your trailer and spotted you, he was usually thinking lunch. But with my size I knew that if a bear stopped by my trailer and spotted *me*, he'd be thinking All-You-Can-Eat Buffet. I wanted to remind Mr. NYC that the Last Frontier wasn't populated with Yogi Bear cartoon characters who wear bow ties and tiptoe into campgrounds with their sidekick Boo-Boo, looking for pic-i-nic baskets. These bears could be dangerous.

As I feared, a large, hungry black bear paid a visit to our campground that very night and finished off the hamburger buns, licked up any remains of fish, and then turned to the New Yorker's camper for more. The bear started pushing on the man's RV, rocking it back and forth, as if he were trying to shake food loose in a vending machine. Inside, the poor guy had awakened and was probably whimpering while curled up in the fetal position behind his three-speed massage recliner with the surround-sound speaker headrest.

Next, the bear started scratching at the trailer like a dog scratching at a back door. A 300-pound dog, that is. With its razor-sharp, can-opener claws, the bear tore into the metal, leaving its mark on the door like a snarling, muscle-bound Zorro. The screech of ripping metal was so horrifying that it made the sound of fingernails across a chalkboard seem like music to the ears.

In the morning, the visibly shaken New Yorker showed up at the door of my trailer wanting to file a complaint. As he whined, I looked down on him from my lofty trailer doorway with a self-satisfied smile and a sense of superiority. I was King of the Campers, and he was a royal pain. I had warned him not to leave food out, so what had happened served him right, I thought self-righteously. In fact, if I had a tablet of the Ten Commandments of Camping handy, I would have conked him on the head with them. "Thou Shalt Not Clean Thy Fish at Thy Campsite" came right after "Thou Shalt Listen to Thy Camp Host."

My smug attitude sent the guy into a rage. If he had had the strength, he probably would have begun shaking my trailer himself.

"Da bears in New York don't act dis way!" he growled.

"Dude, the bears in New York *are in a zoo*!"

"Dat's because they're civilized."

A pregnant pause. I was at a loss for words, so he continued. "All I'm saying is you oughta discipline your bears, buddy."

Discipline my bears? What did he think we were running here—an etiquette school for carnivores? Should we be teaching our grizzlies to clean their claws in a finger bowl after scrounging in the campsite garbage? Or maybe we should be teaching them to pray over their prey before every meal: "Give us this day our daily kill..."

I patted down my pockets, as if hunting for something, before finally responding, "I am all out of sympathy for ignorance, buddy. But here's a piece of advice. Next time, listen to the camp host."

Quickly, I closed my door before this wilderness wannabe showed me his claws.

Later that same morning, I had to alert campers by posting bear warning signs, which specified the date and time of the "visit." It was unsettling knowing that the bear might still be lurking out there somewhere, ready to tap me on the shoulder and ask me if I was the Other White Meat. But I did my duty and posted the warning signs around the camp.

I also made sure I was wearing my "bear bells"—little, tinkling bells strapped to my ankles or wrists or a walking stick so they make noise and keep bears at bay. At first, I had tried to avoid spending good money on bear bells by just babbling to myself out loud while I walked through the woods, hoping it would be enough to scare away bears. But I think the only ones I scared away were campers, who thought I was deranged. So I finally broke down and bought the bear bells. I felt like an overweight Tinker Bell who couldn't get aloft.

Nervously, I went about the camp, posting my warning signs and jingling every step of the way. Fortunately, the black bear didn't return that week, but I stayed on edge, expecting to see him behind every tree.

As the days went by, the Fourth of July eventually arrived, and the park buzzed with activity. With all the fireworks going off, we humans were stupidly signaling to the bears where they could find their next midnight snack. So I shouldn't have been surprised that this turned out to be the day the bear paid us another visit.

The sun had been down for only a couple of hours when the beast struck. This was Alaska in the summer, when the sun goes down around eleven thirty p.m. and it stays dark until about four thirty a.m. It was close to two a.m. when I woke up to the sound of crashing glass. A few cups, which had been perched on my counter to dry, crashed to the floor.

Bear! The bear is shaking my trailer!

Leaping out of bed, I tried to think back on my day, wondering if I had left out food. But that was impossible. I never leave food on my plate—or on any other plates within reach, for that matter. Nevertheless, I became convinced I had done the very thing I lectured the New Yorker about. How could I have been so stupid?

Frantically, I dug out some pots and pans from my cabinet and began banging them together wildly and shouting, "GET AWAY! GET AWAY! SHOO! SHOO!"

Did I really think that saying "Shoo" was going to drive away a big, bad bruin? Nobody likes to be "shooed," least of all an angry, insomniac bear.

After a few minutes, the rocking subsided, so I crawled back into bed, badly shaken. My heart was racing, making sleep impossible, so I lay in bed with my eyes wide open, envisioning the bear ripping open my trailer like a sardine can. *I guess that would make me the sardine*, I thought, and off I went on one of my typical ADHD tangents in which I contemplated the best ways to eat sardines. To me, sardines on saltines were the holy mackerel of snack foods. Sardines in spring water give you omega-3 and a healthy dose of protein and calcium. Another favorite is smearing them with Dijon mustard and tucking them into a nice salad. But the best is...

Bear!

Suddenly, the bear returned with a vengeance, shaking me out of my ADHD daydream. The beast began rocking my world, shaking my trailer the way you might rock a car back and forth to get it out of a snowdrift. So I jumped from my bed, grabbed my collection of pans, and began banging away again. "GO AWAY! GET LOST! I KNOW YOUR MOTHER! SCAT!"

Scat? Did I just tell a bear to scat? Nobody has to tell them to do that. Bears scat naturally. All over the ground.

The night was pure torture. The bear came back a third time to torment me, and once again I had to pull out the pans and make the loudest racket possible. Sometimes, even when the bear wasn't shaking my trailer, I would clang the pans randomly, just to be on the safe side.

Come morning, I was an exhausted, frazzled wreck—but at least my hair looked good. Funny how some details like that never escape you.

The birds were chirping and the morning was clear when I timidly eased open the trailer door and peeked out. No sign of the bear. The creature had scattered some of the paper cups I routinely leave out on my picnic table next to the water jug. Then I noticed a fellow at the campsite next to me, about 30 feet away. He was sitting outside his trailer, brewing coffee over his campfire without a care in the world. If it was safe enough to brew coffee, the bear must have skedaddled. So I strolled over to my neighbor's campsite.

"Did the bear give you any problems last night?" I asked, trying to sound unflustered by the night's events.

The man gave me a sidelong glance. "The what?"

"The bear. Did it give you any problems?"

He stared at me, obviously confused. "Bear? No, I wasn't kept awake by any bears, and the earthquakes didn't keep me awake either. It was *you*, making all that noise! I mean, I like the Fourth of July too, but there comes a point when the celebration is over and ya gotta put the pans down, you know."

I stood there, mouth hanging open. *Earthquakes? Did he just say earthquakes?*

I think my face started turning as red as my hippie hair as it slowly dawned on me. No bear had shaken my trailer last night. It was a series of temblors!

I felt like a complete idiot. Looking back, I should have come up with some reason for my behavior. I could have said that vibrations from the sound of pans banging together counters the seismic waves of earthquakes, but if I said something like that, I suppose he might have considered me even more unstable.

The man just stared at me blankly, and I walked away with my pride badly damaged. Sometimes it feels like my ego is God's piñata.

In a chapter titled "The Great Sin," C.S. Lewis wrote this about pride:

> The essential vice, the utmost evil, is Pride. Unchastity, anger, greed, drunkenness, and all that, are mere fleabites in comparison; it was through Pride that the devil became the devil: Pride leads to every other vice; it is the complete anti-God state of mind.

I couldn't agree more. At the time of the bear incident with the New Yorker, I didn't have very high self-esteem. But self-esteem has nothing to do with pride. You can dislike everything about yourself and still be obsessed with proving that you're better than the next person. In fact, my lack of self-esteem often drove me to look for ways to feed my ego by standing in judgment over people.

When I smugly looked down on my East Coast camp critic, I conveniently forgot that Jesus said, "Judge not, and ye shall not be judged" (Luke 6:37 KJV). And "ye" would be me. While pointing out the speck in the New Yorker's eye with my lofty "I told you so," I didn't even notice the piece of lumber protruding from mine. But the earthquakes did a good job of shattering my ego and putting me in my place.

Arrogance interferes with our relationships with each other, obviously. But even more damaging, it also interferes with our relationship with God. If you're too busy looking down on others, you aren't looking up at the Maker of all things.

At this time of my life, if someone had asked me if I believed in God, I would have said yes. But it was a God of my own making—a touchy-feely God whose job was to make me feel good. Come to think of it, I looked at God as a kind of cosmic recreational vehicle rather than a living, loving person. In this wilderness we call the world, I figured God's job was to make everything comfortable, like the New Yorker's state-of-the-art RV.

But God is the Ultimate Camp Host, and He warns us that life isn't always easy and comfortable and that we need to observe a few rules if we want to survive. I wasn't listening, however. I told God "fuhgeddaboudit" and did whatever I pleased. I didn't want to be subservient to anyone, including the Creator of the universe. I wanted a God who never demanded anything from me.

As an illustration of this attitude, I recently read about fishermen at my old stomping ground at Bird Creek. Evidently, bears were approaching the fishermen and scaring them silly, so the fishermen would toss a fish toward the bear to keep it busy while they ran for safety. The problem is, the bears learned that getting free fish from scared fishermen was easier than hunting for fish themselves. So the bears did less fishing on their own and more chasing fishermen. Why fish when you can get it for free?

That's a perfect picture of where I was at this time spiritually. I didn't want discipline and self-control. I wanted everything tossed my way just like those lazy bears. I wanted to indulge my appetites regardless of the consequences for myself or for others. I turned to food for comfort. About the only thing I didn't swallow was my pride.

Little did I know that things were changing for me during these first wilderness years in Alaska. I can't pinpoint the exact moment I finally gave up my pride and asked God to be Lord of my life. It was a gradual course correction, like turning a huge ocean liner that had been going the wrong direction. But if I had to pick one moment, I suppose it would have been the day I went out to the edge of a small pier at the Bird Creek Campground and had a silent conversation with God. I made it official at a nearby church, answering an altar call and deciding to give it all up—the alcohol, the foul language, the whole lifestyle, kit and caboodle. But more important than these outward expressions, I gave up the pride that kept me foolishly thinking I could get by on my own. It was a quiet conversion, gently nurtured by my buddy Rob's prayers and the obvious magnificence of God's creation all around me.

My conversion may have appeared nondramatic on the outside, but on the inside God was rocking my life like a spiritual earthquake. And when I finally gave up my pride and turned to God on the end of that pier, I had a hunch that a band of angels were banging on their pots and pans and whooping it up as if they were celebrating the Fourth of July and New Year's all wrapped in one. Angels have a way of doing that.

3
OBEDIENCE SCHOOL

I was a man on a mission.

I had driven 45 minutes to the Humane Society in Anchorage to find a dog, unsure of what awaited me. Rob and I had been praying for just the right dog for a long time, so we didn't take this decision lightly. As a new Christian, I had been soaking up many new lessons, and two of the biggest were the power of prayer and the importance of being obedient to God. So Rob and I prayed fervently for a dog.

As I roamed up and down the aisles of the animal shelter, looking into the cages, I was immediately drawn to a five-month-old puppy—part Airedale, part Labrador. He was a bit clumsy with paws so massive that he looked as if he were stumbling around in swimming flippers. Although his clumsiness made him endearing as a puppy, if he continued to walk in that goofy way when he was larger, he would embarrass all of us. But this puppy was so friendly and so smart, I was instantly smitten.

Rob and I were still working as camp hosts at the Bird Creek Campground near Anchorage—two single guys sharing a small camper. We wanted something to show affection to, and it sure wasn't going to be each other, so we decided to get a canine companion. In the cramped quarters of the 21-foot camper, we had a few feet of remaining space, so why not fill it up with a drooling dog?

Actually, our original idea was to get *two* dogs—one for me and one for Rob—and we were going to name them David and Jonathan in honor of the two biblical best friends. But once I saw this black Airedale Lab and considered the space we had available, I decided one dog would be plenty and we would simply share him. I would get 65 of his eventual 130 pounds, and Rob would get the other 65 pounds. I also thought a good name for him would be Samuel because that's the book of the Bible where you can find the story of David and Jonathan.

So right off the bat, on that very first day, I started calling the puppy Sam, Sammy, or Sammers, and the strange thing was that he immediately responded to his name.

Man, he's smart, I thought.

But there were two obstacles to getting Sam.

Obstacle number one: He already had an owner. Sam had been found running loose, so the local animal control had brought him in—for the second time. Before the Humane Society could allow someone to adopt a dog, they had to give an owner seven days to show up and claim the animal, so we would have to wait and see what happened. Also, when the Humane Society puts a dog up for adoption, they start a list, and the person at the top of the list gets first dibs on the dog. But because Sam was not yet up for adoption, no list had been started.

"I know he's got an owner," I told the friendly woman at the shelter, "but just on the off chance that this owner dies in some horrible accident, which I wouldn't wish but wouldn't mind either, could I be the first name on this list?"

I gave her my best sad-puppy face, which I had just learned from the beagle in cage nine.

"All right," she said, probably seeing that it was futile to argue with a man who was acting as desperate as a mutt begging for scraps. "But don't get your hopes up. If the owner shows up anytime in the next seven days, the dog goes back to him."

Obstacle number two was Rob. When I left for the shelter, Rob made it crystal clear he wanted a dog that had a tail and that hadn't been "fixed." So Sam had two strikes against him. His tail had been cropped—a common procedure with Airedales—and the shelter required that all dogs be fixed before they're released.

But there was just something about Sam. So I called Rob on his cell phone and told him to get down to the shelter as soon as he could and check out the dogs during his lunch break.

"Did you see one you liked?" he asked.

I paused. "I'd rather not say."

"You'd rather not say?"

"If this dog is really an answer to our prayers, I want God to direct you to him."

"So it's a *him*?"

"For now. But he'll be an 'it' before he gets released. The point is, my lips are sealed."

"Whatever."

I wouldn't even give Rob a hint because I thought that if he picked out Sam without any prodding from me, I would know this dog was the one. So Rob went down to the Humane Society shelter, and pretty soon I received a phone call.

"There isn't anything here that really interests me," he said, and immediately my spirit deflated. I was crestfallen. I had been so sure!

But then he continued.

"However, there is a pretty friendly black Lab here. He doesn't have a tail, but there's something about him."

I nearly jumped through the phone. "That's Sam!" I shouted. "Quick! I already started a list, but if you put your name on it, you'll increase our odds of getting him." I figured that if they didn't reach me by phone, they might get ahold of Rob if he was next on the list.

There had to be close to 50 dogs in the shelter, and Rob had picked out Sam. What were the odds? But still, we had to wait for seven long days. The length of creation itself.

Each morning, I headed down to the shelter, and when I called out Sam's name, he instantly responded. Amazing! Then I would camp out in front of Sam's cage, sitting on the floor and feeding him biscuits and other treats while people had to step around me as they shuffled by. After an hour-long visit, I would head back to the camp, where I kept my eyes peeled for any food scraps the campers left around that I could feed to Sam—fish, hamburger, roasted chicken, or hot dogs. I avoided the tofu because, as I said, Sam was a smart dog.

Meanwhile, Rob would go to the animal shelter during his lunch hour to visit Sam and teach him basic tricks. Every day, around noon, Sam would be staring at the door, as if he could read a clock, and he would go nuts when he saw Rob appear.

The shelter lady was astounded by the attention we gave him.

"In all the years I've worked here, we've never had anybody come and do this," she said. "You guys deserve this dog."

As the days ticked by, Sam's adoption list grew and grew, and pretty soon there were close to three dozen names on the sheet. Sam had become the most popular dog in the shelter. But each day, I dreaded receiving The Call—the phone call from the shelter saying Sam's owner had showed up.

At long last, day seven arrived.

I don't think I had ever worked as quickly as I did that morning, checking in campers. I flew through my duties and was getting ready to jump into the truck for the drive to Anchorage when it happened. We received The Call.

"I have some news for you," said the shelter lady, and I could hear the disappointment in her voice. My heart began to teeter on the edge, about to drop. Then she lowered the boom.

"The dog's owner came in," she said.

I could hear my heart hit the floor with a thud.

But she went on. The woman said that Sam's owner had arrived at the shelter drunk and abusive. He yelled at Sam, and then he started shouting at the lady when he found out he would have to pay a fine. This was the second time Sam had been brought in as a stray, and that meant the owner would have to pay $100 to get his dog back.

"I'm not paying that much for that stupid dog!" he bellowed. "You can give the dog to whoever wants it."

Gladly, she was probably thinking.

The owner had to sign over his rights to Sam, and when he was done filling out the form, he threw the clipboard across the counter. Noticing that he had neglected to write down his dog's name, the lady handed him back the clipboard, and he scribbled out Sam's real name so angrily that he nearly ripped through the paper with the pen.

When she told me Sam's real name, I was stunned. The man called him Hammer, but he sometimes referred to him as Ham or Hammy. So that explained why he responded to the names I had been using!

Ham, Hammer, and Hammy had become Sam, Sammers, and Sammy. Like Saul using his Greek name, Paul, when he began his evangelistic journeys, this gregarious Labrador was embarking on a new life with a new name and a new identity.

I have had many dogs over the years, but never one like Sam. He was friendly, obedient, loving, and incredibly smart—a clear answer to prayer. Rob took him to obedience school (something my parents probably wished I could have attended), and he became the model of the faithful canine. Sam could do so much more than the basic sit, stay, or fetch. If I told him to get my shoes, he knew from the scent which ones were my mine and which ones were Rob's. (I'm certain Rob's smelled worse.) But even more than that, Sam could *anticipate* what I was going to ask him to do. He was extremely observant and followed my gaze. As a result, he would sometimes fetch the thing I wanted even before I had a chance to give the command.

Sam also knew his right from his left, so we could just say, "Turn left," and he would do it. He could respond to hand signals from 100 yards away. We could motion for him to sit, and he would sit. And if a ball rolled into the street, he didn't dash after it. He knew better. He just stared at the ball, thinking, *Poor, sad ball*, as it was crushed by a passing car. He was that obedient.

In addition, Sam was sensitive. I still remember the day I received a phone call telling me that my grandmother had passed away. Sam was in the other room, but somehow he sensed how I was feeling because he immediately dashed to my side and began to nuzzle against me before I had even hung up the phone.

Sam was the most obedient of dogs, but he wasn't perfect. One day, Rob and Sam were out exploring. Rob pulled the Jeep up to a dramatic overlook at a lake, but when he opened the door, a ball accidentally tumbled out and rolled straight toward a clump of bushes. Sam knew better than to chase a ball into the street, but we had no rules about chasing balls into bushes.

"No!" Rob shouted.

Sam didn't stop.

"Sam, stop! No!"

Sam bolted through the bushes, and just like that, he was gone.

Rob had desperately shouted "No!" because he knew that just on the other side of the bushes was a steep cliff—an almost 120-foot drop into the lake below. It was slanted just enough that Sam would probably bounce off outcroppings several times on the way down. If he survived, he would be a badly broken dog.

Sam had completely vanished, so Rob took off running down a pathway that led to the lake. It wasn't until he got almost all the way down that he could look back up and see what had happened.

It was a miracle.

The biggest outcropping on the cliff face was a ledge, only about one foot wide and three feet long. Somehow, Sam had fallen directly onto this tiny ledge. He seemed to be all right, but now the question was, how in the world was Rob going to get him down from the ledge? The top of the cliff was about 30 feet above Sam, and the lake was about 90 feet below.

So Rob climbed up. Finding footholds and handholds, he slowly worked his way up the side of the cliff. He had experience as a rock climber, but he had no ropes or other equipment with him. And when he finally reached the ledge, he was faced with yet another puzzle—how to get off the ledge with a 130-pound dog.

Rob considered picking up Sam and then leaping together into the freezing cold lake below. But that posed too many risks. They would probably hit several outcroppings on the way down, breaking bones and possibly skulls. Besides, even if they successful reached the water without killing themselves, there was no place where Sam could climb out.

There was only one way out of their predicament—up.

So Rob groaned as he lifted his huge dog to chest level. Then he pinned Sam between the cliff wall and his chest, and he pulled himself up a few inches using the nearest handhold. Pausing, he nudged Sam up another half a foot or so, still keeping him pinned between his chest and the cliff. Then Rob found another handhold and pulled himself up another half a foot. He did this again and again with a large, squirming dog pressed against his chest and a deadly drop beneath him.

For most people, just climbing up 30 feet without ropes would be freaky enough. Try doing it with a large dog pinned between your chest and the cliff.

Muscles aching, Rob continued to inch his way upward like a slow-moving Spider-Man. But the most difficult and dangerous maneuver awaited him near the top. When Rob finally approached the summit, he noticed a slight overhang at the top of the cliff. He wouldn't be able to push Sam straight up and over the ledge. He had to lean back to be able to push Sam safely onto the top of the cliff.

Lean back? How in the world could he do that without tumbling backward off the cliff face?

Rob looked down. He had no choice but to try.

So while pinned against the cliff, he carefully raised Sam higher and higher until he was holding the 130-pound dog directly above his head. Then, with Sam's legs pedaling the air and trying to get purchase on the grassy ledge above, Rob leaned back and shoved with all of his might. It would be so easy for him to lose his balance and tumble 120 feet down.

But Sam made it to safety, and Rob climbed the last few feet alone.

This story is the perfect parable of our lives and the temptations surrounding us every day. The ball that Sam chased out of the car is like sin. It looks so appealing, so much fun, that we will sometimes chase it right off the edge of a cliff. Living with no boundaries and no rules might sound like paradise to some people, but we live in a fallen universe, and God has reasons for His rules. He sees the dangers we are blinded to, and He sets boundaries for our own protection. God establishes these limits but not because He is an ogre. He sets them because He loves us that much.

In fact, His barriers give us more freedom, not less. When you have a barrier, a guardrail at the edge of a cliff, you can move around with more abandon because the fence keeps you safe. It's like that with God's boundaries, God's guardrails. They give us the security to fully enjoy life without the terror of going over the edge. And if we ever go running off the cliff in our pursuit of sin, God will do whatever it takes to carry us back up, like the Good Shepherd carrying a lost sheep on his shoulders—or Rob inching Sam up a cliff.

The temptation of sin is strong, but it is a trap—every bit as deceptive and dangerous as the traps set by Eskimos to kill wolves. When an Eskimo wants to kill a wolf, he soaks his knife in the blood of a seal and lets it freeze. Then he soaks the knife in more seal blood and lets it freeze again. He keeps repeating the pattern. Soak the knife in blood. Let it freeze. Soak the knife in blood. Let it freeze.

Finally, he is left with a thick, frozen "bloodsicle." The Eskimo then jams the knife into the ground and waits. Drawn by the scent of the blood, a wolf will inevitably wander by and begin licking the frozen blood on the blade. But as he licks and licks and licks, the frozen blood makes the wolf's tongue so numb that the wolf doesn't even notice when he licks his way down to the knife and begins to cut himself on the blade. He just keeps licking, slits his tongue, and doesn't realize the blood he is lapping up is now his own.

The wolf bleeds to death, and the Eskimo finds the carcass only a few feet from the knife.

Sin is many layered, it is attractive, and it tastes good—like blood on a knife. But the more we indulge in it, the more we become numb to sin, and we don't even notice the damage it is doing to us. The thing that delighted us eventually kills us.

I don't always like the limits God puts on my life, but I have to trust and obey. God doesn't put us on leashes, so it's up to us to keep from running after the deadly things that look so innocent and appealing. We live in a dangerous world, and we all need someone looking out for us. We all need someone who will go to any length to rescue us. We all need someone who will sacrifice himself on a cliff or on a cross to bring us back to solid ground.

The good news is that we do have that Someone—if we just listen for our Master's voice. And obey.

4 THE DEVIL WEARS DENIM

The church usher was all smiles as he led me toward a door off to the right.

"Let me find you a place where you'll be comfortable," he said, flashing his teeth and escorting me through the door and up the stairs to a large balcony overlooking the main sanctuary of this gorgeous church.

Then he was gone, leaving me in the balcony with only two other people. As I looked over at my balcony mates—one man and one woman—I got a strange feeling that something wasn't quite right. The first guy had long hair and a long beard, and he wore jeans and a cut-off denim vest. Tattoos covered both of his arms like ink shirtsleeves. The woman had a swath of her hair dyed bright pink, and she sported a piercing on her chin and a large nose ring with a chain that extended to her pierced ear.

Before I could fully process all this, the usher was back, escorting yet another man into our midst. He wore a black-checkered flannel shirt, jeans, and a baseball hat.

"It looks like you're more ready for fishing than church," said the smiling usher to the man. "You might want to rethink the jeans next time."

I thought his comment was a little out of line, borderline rude, and 100 percent judgmental. Shrugging it off, I imagined that if anyone took a good hard look at my compatriots in the balcony, they might wonder, *What's with all the weirdoes?* But then it occurred to me. I too was one of the weirdoes, at least in the eyes of this zealous usher. I was wearing my tan Carhartt overalls, which had become my official uniform since coming to Alaska. (I owned seven pairs of tan Carhartt overalls, one for each day of the week, all purchased at Mr. Brewster's store.) I was also overweight and had a scruffy beard and long, red hair streaming down past my shoulders, so I had a feeling that the others in the balcony were staring at *me* and wondering, *What in the world am I doing with this long-haired misfit?*

Staring down on the church's main level, I noticed that everybody was well manicured with perfect hair and suits and ties. Suddenly, it all became crystal clear. This church televised their services, and being in the balcony put us far away from the roving eye of the TV camera. They were probably worried that the pious viewers at home would be watching on TV, and as the camera slowly panned the congregation, Mrs. Pious would say to Mr. Pious, "Oh look at all the pretty people...AHHHHH!" When the camera suddenly landed on me, grinning in my big tan overalls, she would scream as loudly as Kevin McCallister on *Home Alone* and go running out of the room.

Was that what the church usher was trying to prevent?

So I sat in the balcony, fuming. The pastor's sermon was quite good, but it was hard to absorb the message when I had received another message loud and clear. My fellow misfits and I had been told that we weren't ready for prime time. We weren't perfect enough to show up on the church's TV broadcast.

As I sat there, I took my pen and scratched the words "judge mental" on the corner of my church bulletin. I accidentally separated the two words, "judge" and "mental," as I paused to get more ink flowing in my ballpoint pen. But separating those words conjured up an imaginary character I wound up calling Judge Mental. He rules in the court of popular church opinion, but this court has no jury because everyone knows you can't get 12 people in a church to agree on anything. The verdict was in. We had been condemned by Judge Mental—banished to exile in the balcony.

When I thought about the usher telling the flannel-shirt man to rethink the jeans, I puzzled over his reasoning. Did he think "denim" was evil because it begins with "d" and has the same number of letters as "devil" or "demon"?

I knew for a fact that this church had issues with denim because I once gave a pretty Winnie-the-Pooh denim dress to the daughter of some good friends. The little girl attended a school run by this church, and when she showed up to class, so proud of her new dress, the principal called the parents and told them to bring over a different dress for their daughter. Maybe the principal thought the girl might become denim possessed.

This usher looked at the flannel-shirt man as if he too were denim possessed. But what if this man didn't own anything other than a few pairs of well-worn jeans? Or what if he was out fishing and suddenly felt God urging him to put down his fishing rod and spontaneously head to church for the first time in years? Would he ever come back to church again?

We are called to be fishers of men, but this church usher had decided to throw a few of the fish back.

I was angry. I had recently rededicated my life to the Lord, so I tried not to let this experience sour that transformation. I shook off the dust as I departed this church and continued to look for a congregation to call home.

As "floating camp hosts," Rob and I filled in at three primary campgrounds—Bird Creek, Eagle River, and Eklutna Lake. We replaced the regular camp hosts whenever they were gone, so we bounced from camp to camp. We spent most of our time at Bird Creek, but when we finally had a chance to do a stint at the remote Eklutna Lake Campground, the ranger was nice enough to give me a brief tour of the area. Eklutna Lake Campground was close to the municipality of Eagle River, and I still had church hunting on my mind as we passed through this area.

"I don't suppose you'd know if there's a good church around here, would ya?" I asked the ranger as we came around a bend on Eagle River Loop Road.

"I don't go to church," said the ranger, "but there's a big red one just ahead that I pass by every day." He pointed to a large, red, barn-like church on the left.

I made a mental note of it.

That night, Rob returned home from his new job as a security service technician, and I told him about the big red church.

"Okay, do you want to check it out tonight?" Rob asked. It was a Wednesday, when most churches have their midweek services.

There's no time like the present, so we hopped into the Jeep and drove to the red church. From the moment we walked through the door, we sensed something different. We weren't shuffled to a balcony or some other Siberian outpost within the church. We sat on the left side, about halfway down, and we soaked up the pastor's eloquent sermon. When the service was over, all kinds of people welcomed us, including the pastor, Jack Aiken. After greeting Rob and me, he spent the next 15 minutes showing genuine interest in us. Where were we from? What brought us to Alaska? It was obvious from our dress that we were not prospective wealthy contributors to the church coffers. From outward appearances, we had nothing to offer. But Pastor Aiken wasn't interested in what we looked like on the outside or what we could give him. He was just interested in us.

Jesus was like that, attracting tax collectors and prostitutes and demon-possessed women (and maybe even some denim-possessed women) into His following—not the kind of people you want showing up on your church television program. If Jesus had a television show, and if the camera had landed on Mary Magdalene, I imagine a lot of Pharisees watching back at home would have leaped from their recliners, screamed, and torn their garments.

We fell in love with King's Way Church, and for the next four weeks we were at every service on Wednesday night, Sunday morning, and Sunday night. But as floating hosts, we knew that our stay at the Eklutna Lake Campground was only temporary, and soon we would be back at Bird Creek, much too far away to keep attending King's Way. The drive from Bird Creek to church could be as long as two or three hours—seven hours if there was an accident along what was known as the Highway of Death. This winding two-lane road is sandwiched between Cook Inlet on one side and a mountain on the other. Drivers sometimes become so enthralled by watching whales on one side and mountain goats on the other that they either drive off the road or into each other. Hence the Highway of Death.

With such a formidable distance between Bird Creek and the church in Eagle River, we were crushed that we couldn't keep attending King's Way. So Rob and I turned to prayer. I asked God if He could maneuver things so the regular hosts at Eklutna Lake Campground would be willing to trade assignments. They could take Bird Creek, and we would remain where we were.

But God didn't answer that prayer—at least not in the way we expected.

The very next day, the ranger approached us with a new opportunity.

"A lot of teens have been wreaking havoc, vandalizing the Briggs Bridge site," he said. Briggs Bridge was a day-use facility, which meant it was closed at night, making it the perfect location for rebellious teens to party parent-free.

"Would you two be willing to stay at the Briggs Bridge day-use facility for the rest of the season?" he asked. We would become the enforcers, keeping the rowdies out at night.

"Where is it located?" I asked.

And then the ranger floored me. "You remember that big red church I pointed out to you a while back?" he asked.

"Yeah."

"Well, Briggs Bridge is just down the road from it."

As the ranger drove me to Briggs Bridge, I couldn't stop smiling. We discovered that we could even see the tip-top of the King's Way steeple from the park entrance. It was that close. As if that weren't amazing enough, because the day-use facility closed in the evening, we had it to ourselves every night, although it took a bit of work to finally stop the teens from showing up with their beer. The park provided plenty of room for Sam to run—it was like having our own personal Frontierland without the rides.

But best of all, we could continue attending Pastor Aiken's church, only a half mile away. In fact, I found myself regularly dropping in to the church, either to talk to the pastor or just to pray in the sanctuary. The church secretary, Janie, also made a point of inviting me over for every staff birthday celebration because she knew I loved my sugar.

From this experience, I learned that God doesn't just answer prayer. He sometimes *exceeds* our measly requests so that our cup runneth over. We had been praying to switch places with the Eklutna camp hosts, but God was thinking, *Silly boys. I'm going to set up your new home right next to that church.* He was going to put us in a place where the gates close at night and the six of us could spend quality time together—the Holy Trinity of Father, Son, and Holy Spirit, and the Three Stooges of Rob, me, and Sam.

King's Way became our home—and a place of complete acceptance.

As I mentioned earlier, I'd had a major change of heart and given up many of my bad habits—drugs and alcohol—but I still smoked cigarettes. In fact, after answering that altar call, I went straight outside to contemplate my rebirth and immediately lit up a cigarette. Exhaling a puff of smoke, I thought, *Whew, that was close*. I felt I had dodged an eternal destination in a place where you could always turn to the devil and ask, "You got a light?"

My cigarette habit was a constant embarrassment to me, which was why I concealed the smelly habit by popping breath fresheners. I did just about everything except take a bath in a tub of aftershave. So when Pastor Aiken asked one day if I wanted to join the church choir, I averted my eyes, turned bright red, and mumbled, "Sorry, but I can't."

Puzzled, he stared at me.

After taking a deep breath, I added, "I can't be in the choir because I smoke cigarettes."

A long uncomfortable pause followed. Pastor Aiken cocked his head and just kept staring at me. Finally, he spoke. "You're not planning on smoking cigarettes in choir, are you?"

I was stunned by his response. "No," I said.

Immediately, my imagination began running wild (as it often did), and I pictured myself trying to sing, "Clap Your Hands, All You People" with a cigarette in my hand. I then started wondering what would happen if the church created a smoking section in their lobby and called it the Great Cloud of Witnesses.

"Torry," Pastor Aiken said. "*Torry*."

I snapped back to reality. Pastor Aiken then explained that they had people in the choir with all kinds of issues, including drinking problems, and that the church was where you come to get better. It's like Jesus said in Mark 2:17: "It is not the healthy who need a doctor, but the sick. I have not come to call the righteous, but sinners."

Jesus also had plenty to say about the Judge Mentals of his day—the Pharisees, the kind of people who think church is for the righteous only. He called the Pharisees whitewashed tombs, which was quite a biting insult in its day. During the last month of the liturgical year, *Adar*, Jewish families whitewashed the stone monuments marking graves or tombs. According to the Talmud, the authoritative commentary on the Jewish Law, whitewashing was necessary to warn people to stay away because any contact with a dead person (even a gravestone) would make them ritually unclean. The white stones alerted people and prevented them from accidentally walking on a grave. Jesus referred to this in Matthew 23:27-28.

> Woe to you, teachers of the law and Pharisees, you hypocrites! You are like whitewashed tombs, which look beautiful on the outside but on the inside are full of the bones of the dead and everything unclean. In the same way, on the outside you appear to people as righteous but on the inside you are full of hypocrisy and wickedness.

In the first church where I began this tale, the usher "whitewashed" the congregation's appearance by putting only the beautiful Christians in front of the TV camera while hiding the weirdoes like me. But at Pastor Aiken's church, we were no longer considered "unclean," even while wearing Carhartt overalls. We weren't banished from view or told to rethink the jeans. The church wasn't embarrassed to embrace us. They even wanted me in their choir, and I can't help but sing the praises of that kind of church.

They chose the way of Jesus. They chose the King's Way.

5
GHOST FISH

Something was definitely wrong with this bald eagle.

Rob and I edged closer and closer to the massive bird, getting about 15 feet away, and yet it continued to just stand there, aware of our presence but doing nothing. Each of us was armed with only a blanket, and we approached from different angles.

Still, the eagle remained firmly grounded, cocking its head and giving us a good hard look.

Normally, a human cannot get nearly this close to a bald eagle without it taking off and soaring away. It had to be sick. At least that's what the campers who had spotted this eagle told us. So, being dutiful camp hosts at the Briggs Bridge day-use facility northeast of Anchorage, Rob and I hiked about two miles down a trail into the wilderness, following the campers' directions, and found the poor eagle just where they said—along a narrow creek branching off the appropriately named Eagle River.

Rob was the brains of our operation, and he suggested we bring along blankets to throw over the eagle so we could carry it to Dr. James R. Scott, a renowned Anchorage veterinarian who founded the

Bird Treatment and Learning Center in 1988. Dr. Scott had built up quite a reputation for rehabilitating injured and sick birds.

We crept to within about seven feet of the eagle, but still it did not budge. Very strange.

The blankets would protect us from the double threat of the eagle's talons and beak. Bald eagles have a hooked yellow beak, ideal for ripping into prey and unsuspecting camp hosts. Also, each foot is equipped with four sharp talons that can clamp down like a vise on its prey and camp-host appendages. This bird was huge. It stood more than two feet tall and had a wingspan of close to eight feet.

Rob may have been the brains of the outfit, but neither of us had thought very far ahead. Even if we got this eagle in our blankets, how in the world were we going to transport it to Dr. Scott? Were we going to trudge two miles back to our camper with an angry bird in our arms? Oblivious to this part of the plan, we continued to inch forward. Now we were only a few feet away. Slowly, we started to raise our blankets. On Rob's signal, we would throw the blankets over the eagle in unison, and hopefully we wouldn't get a face full of angry eagle in the process. But as we moved in a little bit closer, the eagle finally budged.

It hopped away.

That's all it did. The eagle didn't fly away. It didn't even try flapping its huge wings. It simply hopped away, as if it were perched on an invisible pogo stick.

Rob and I exchanged looks. Shrugging, we slowly approached once again.

The eagle hopped back once again.

By this time, I noticed that two other eagles were positioned close by and watching everything unfold—probably the bird's buddies. I had a sneaking suspicion that the two eagle friends were snickering at us. In fact, I think the sick eagle might also have been in on the joke because every time we got within a few feet, the eagle hopped away as if he were taunting us.

Finally, we had him backed up all the way to the creek. The whole scene was beginning to unfold like the climax of dozens of police shows where the officer slowly and carefully approaches the crazed killer who is waving a loaded gun.

"Take it easy, buddy, and no one will get hurt."

I didn't actually say those words, but I might have if this had been the climax of an episode of *NCIS: Alaska*.

Again, Rob and I raised our blankets, ready to pounce. Then, at long last, the eagle did something that no perp on *NCIS* had ever done. He flapped his wings and flew to the other side of the creek. He didn't get much lift—just enough to get away from these annoying humans. I shot a look at the other two eagles, still perched nearby. They were definitely laughing at us.

Something was fishy about the whole situation—and that's when we spotted it. Fish bones were scattered everywhere on the ground along the creek. It was like some cult mass suicide where dozens and dozens of fish drank the Kool-Aid together.

Rob and I looked up toward the eagle, which was still standing on the other side of the creek.

We realized this was no sick eagle. This was a *fat* eagle!

Judging by all the bones, the eagle must have been gorging himself on salmon all morning until he was so bloated and stuffed that he couldn't get off the ground. Not until we had him cornered did the bird finally muster the strength to rise from the ground and wobble to safety, his belly filled to the brim with salmon.

Most of us know the story of how salmon spawn, so I'll just review the basics. When salmon prepare to spawn, they swim upriver against the current, and then they wiggle down a creek, returning to the same place where they were born. There, in a few inches of water, they lay their eggs, which are fertilized by the male, and then they die.

That's right. They just keel over and die.

But they don't expire all at once. If you spot a salmon that has just laid eggs, you might notice that it's half alive. You might see some little twitches, like a person in a Civil War reenactment going overboard with his death scene, twitching and flopping around for added drama. When they're twitching like that, half alive and half dead, people around here call them "ghost fish." They're like the walking dead (or the swimming dead). Zombie fish.

Our eagle friend had evidently stumbled across an entire all-you-can-eat buffet of tasty ghost fish twitching and flopping around in the shallow creek. Keep in mind that a typical king salmon can weigh between 30 and 50 pounds, so that's a lot of fish. This eagle ate and ate and ate—kind of like your Uncle Maury at Thanksgiving eating so much turkey that he can't get out of his recliner. But this time, the bird was doing all the eating, and he couldn't get off the ground—until he became desperate.

I know a lot of Christians like that.

Some Christians take in a lot of spiritual food—massive amounts of Christian teaching, which is a good thing. No problem there. But for some Christians, that's all they do—take in information. They're comfortable sitting in the pew, absorbing lessons and spitting out the bones, but they don't put the teachings of Jesus into action. Christ told us to be fishers of men, but if we're not careful we can become lazy and overstuffed and too comfortable to get out into the world and do any actual fishing.

Upon reflection, I also realized that before I came to Alaska and recommitted my life to the Lord, I was a bit like the ghost fish. I was only half alive. I had enough church experience to know how to go through the motions and do just enough twitching to show that I might be spiritually alive. I was a zombie Christian, putting on an act, but I was dead inside. My buddy Rob was different. He spoke the words, and he meant them. He carried around his Bible, but it wasn't just a prop to look holier than thou. He read his Bible continuously, and at first it bugged the life out of me. Rob didn't just devour teachings and loll around like an overstuffed eagle; he put the teachings of Christ into motion. In fact, sometimes his willingness to leap into action to help people put him in harm's way, as happened in another incident along Eagle River around the same time.

The McGuires, a wonderful family of four, had been out canoeing when their boat capsized. It was summer in Alaska, but you have to understand that the Eagle River is fed by a glacier, so the water is dangerously cold all year round. The mother, Sylvia, later told me that hitting the water took their breath away, and they came out of the water gasping as their lungs closed down. Knowing they had to find warmth soon, they ditched the canoe along the bank. Micah, the teen, lost his glasses in the water, and his younger sister, Shannon, lost her boots, so her father, Pat, had to carry her through the forest to the highway. Then they drove to the Briggs Bridge day-use facility and showed up at our camper, soaked to the bone and freezing cold.

"Can you get ahold of a ranger or someone to retrieve our canoe?" asked Pat.

Rob didn't wait a beat. "We don't need to bother the ranger. I've got a wet suit. I can float down the river and get it for you."

Rob's idea caught me off guard. It seemed like a good solution in theory, but the problem was that the wet suit was designed for Florida. It was made to keep a person warm down to water temperatures of 50 to 60 degrees Fahrenheit, but this water was probably 35 to 38 degrees. It was near the freezing point!

"Rob, don't you think that's a little dangerous?" I asked.

"Stop freaking out."

"Yeah, but I don't think—"

Before I could finish my sentence, he was already pulling out his wet suit.

Nothing I could say would deter Rob from an adventure, so I drove him ten miles upriver, where he plunged into the frigid water. The water was a shock to his system to say the least. A wet suit works by allowing in a thin layer of water between a person's body and the wet suit. The body eventually warms up the thin insulating layer of water next to the skin, but initially it's freezing. In this kind of water, it takes your breath away. Even worse, whenever you move, the wet suit pumps fresh water into the suit—fresh *freezing* water. So Rob alternated swimming and floating on his back as he was carried down the Eagle River. He knew that he could stand about a half hour in the water before hypothermia set in.

Personally, I thought he was taking his job as a floating camp host a little too literally. I was terrified. Why in the world would he risk hypothermia for a canoe? It wasn't like it was made out of chocolate.

And then there were the bears. This area was flush with all kinds of bears, including grizzlies. You were not even advised to walk alone in this area, let alone float alone down a river, where you might encounter a couple of grizzlies in the water fishing for salmon. Wrapped in his wet suit, Rob looked like a sausage, all snug and tight in his sausage casing—the perfect grizzly hors d'oeuvre.

It also occurred to Rob that he might not be able to spot the canoe along the bank as he went floating by, carried by a fast-moving current. He estimated that the canoe was about a mile down the river, and he figured he would find it, hop in the canoe, and paddle the last nine miles. But if he missed the canoe, he could wind up floating the entire ten miles. These were the kinds of thoughts meandering through Rob's mind as he came around a bend, floating on his back, and spotted a couple of fishermen on the bank.

"Hello!" he called out cheerily, waving at them. "Have you seen a canoe anywhere along the bank?"

The fishermen must have been thunderstruck. Here they were, calmly fishing, and this crazy guy in a wet suit comes zipping by, floating on his back and asking about a canoe!

"Have a nice day!" Rob called out before disappearing around the next bend.

Meanwhile, I was back at our campground, fretting and pulling out my hair. One hour went by. Two hours. If Rob didn't show up, how in the world would we be able to find him? When I told the park ranger what Rob had done, he was initially pretty mad. But then he kind of perked up, probably thinking he might have a rescue on his hands. Maybe he was excited by the idea of finally seeing some action after spending so much time checking in campers and telling them where they can find the closest store to buy s'mores ingredients.

Three hours went by. Still no word from Rob. Had he frozen to death? Had he become a frozen Robsicle for a hungry, grumpy bear?

Little did I know that Rob was having a grand old time. Even though the water was close to freezing, the air temperature was in the seventies—a beautiful, sunny day. He spotted the canoe tucked in among some brush on the bank, so he climbed aboard and began paddling down the rest of the stretch to Briggs Bridge. However, maneuvering the winding river was taking longer than he had anticipated, and overheating now became his biggest problem. Paddling a canoe in a wet suit with the air temperature in the seventies can get you heated pretty quickly.

I still don't think risking hypothermia to rescue a canoe was a smart thing to do. But Rob had an adventurous streak that bordered on recklessness, and he loved helping people. He was like the apostle Peter in that way. Peter had his issues, but he was a risk taker. Sure, he could be a bit reckless and impulsive, but his holy spontaneity must have made Jesus smile. In Matthew 14, when Jesus approached the disciples' boat by walking on water, what did Peter do? He said to Jesus, "Lord, if it's you, tell me to come to you on the water."

Jesus responded with one word: "Come."

I wonder if Peter was shocked by that one word. Most of us might stammer, "Uh...I didn't really mean it...not literally."

But Peter was game, and he climbed out of the boat with no wet suit, no canoe...not even a pair of water wings. His faith was not half dead as mine once was. He wasn't a ghost fish, nor was he a fat eagle, too comfortable to move, too complacent to care. Peter scrambled out of that comfortable boat and did a bit of strolling on the water before the wind scared him to death and he began to sink. But give him credit. How many of us have walked on water? How many of us would have even considered jumping out of that boat?

When Jesus rose from the dead, He appeared to the disciples. In the account in John 21, the disciples were busy fishing when they spotted a man on the shore, and one of them exclaimed, "It is the Lord!"

What did Peter do? He dove into the water and swam for shore. Peter was so drawn to Jesus that he wasn't about to wait for the boat to reach shore to be with Him. He hurled himself into the water. Are we drawn that powerfully to God? Would we jump into the Sea of Galilee just to get close to Jesus?

Peter was a holy risk taker—and so is my buddy Rob. Peter was always leaping—jumping out of boats or leaping into action with his sword when his Lord was threatened in the Garden of Gethsemane. Although Jesus rebuked him for using his sword in the Garden, I think the Lord loved Peter's boldness. No wonder Jesus called him "the rock" and built His church on Peter's shoulders. Leaders take risks, and Peter had no trouble taking risks. We don't need to take *foolish* risks, but we do need to get out and do something bold.

If you simply feel too tired or apathetic to leap into action, know this. Isaiah 40:29,31 says that God "gives strength to the weary and increases the power of the weak...those who hope in the LORD will renew their strength. They will soar on wings like eagles."

It's true. We can all soar—if we just put down that 50-pound salmon and try.

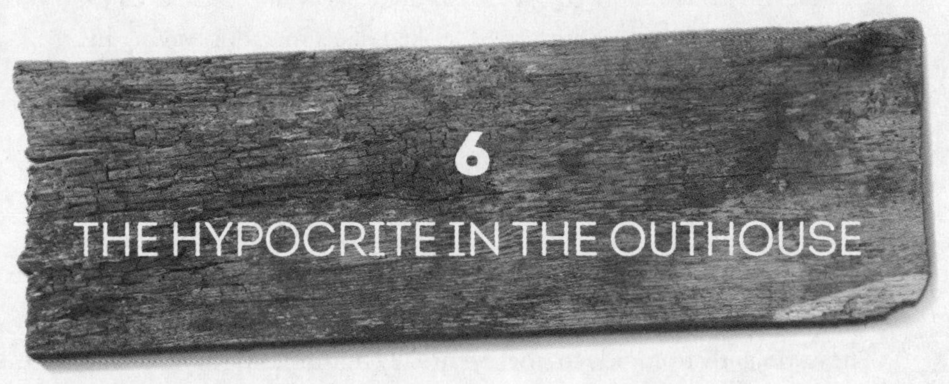

6
THE HYPOCRITE IN THE OUTHOUSE

I didn't like the way the mountain goat was eyeing me.

Three mountain goats had wandered into the Bird Creek Campground, and as camp host, it was my job to shoo them away. Mountain goats will eat anything in sight because everything looks like a bag of cookies to them, so you don't want them in the camp, chewing on hiking shoes and using tent ropes to floss their teeth. But as I began to wave my arms and make shooing sounds, one of the goats got very irritated. He was showing signs of dominance—head lowered, ears back. It was the kind of look I used to get from high school seniors who wanted to stuff me inside a locker. (That never happened, thankfully, probably because they knew I'd never fit.)

The goat sported a pair of wicked horns, so when he started to charge at me, I backed away, hands held out in defense. Suddenly, I was the one being shooed away. I looked around for anyplace I could run to for safety, but all I could see nearby was the outhouse.

The mountain goat made another charge, and I backpedaled once again. This time, he got so close that I put my hands at the base of his horns and shoved him back. He didn't like that one bit.

Next, I slowly removed my Alaska State Parks jacket to wave him off, but instead it egged him on. I looked like a matador waving his cape in front of a bull. That did it. Now the goat was *really* ticked. He charged, and as he ran past I stepped to the side and draped my coat in front of his face.

Olé!

Only one tiny problem...my coat snagged on his horns, and he whisked it out of my hands. Suddenly, the goat had a coat draped over his head, blinding him, and he was beyond bonkers. He shook his head violently from side to side, eventually hurling aside my coat and turning on me with fire in his eyes. This goat clearly had no respect for authority. He couldn't possibly have missed seeing the words ALASKA STATE PARKS emblazoned on the back of my coat. With the coat draped over his head, the words were right in front of him!

After flinging aside the jacket, the goat faced me squarely and locked eyes on me—like a heat-seeking missile locking onto its target. This time, I had no jacket to use as a matador's cape.

When he charged again, I had no other choice. I made a mad dash for the outhouse, leaped inside, and slammed the door shut just before the goat crashed headfirst against it.

BAM!

As everyone knows, the idea behind an outhouse is to use it as quickly as humanly possible because it is universally recognized as one of the foulest places on the entire planet. That's probably why they call it an "out" house—you want to get out of there as soon as you can. I breathed through my mouth and listened at the door. I didn't hear any goat noises, so it seemed safe. Carefully, I cracked open the door...and saw the goat glaring back at me from about five feet away.

He charged. I slammed the door shut with a BANG.

The goat answered with a BAM!

When I opened the door for that brief moment, I had caught a glimpse of a group of campers in the distance. I think they had gathered to watch their fearless camp host cornered in an outhouse. I could hear murmuring and giggles, which I assumed were human sounds because I don't think goats are capable of giggling—although if they ever were, this would be the moment. I imagined several of the campers setting up their chairs, munching potato chips, and leaning back with a cool drink. This standoff was as entertaining as anything they would see all week.

Once again I edged open the door, and once again the goat charged. BAM!

The outhouse was sturdy, built on concrete, so I wasn't afraid the goat would plow it over. But I began to wonder if the door would hold out. I also wondered if my stomach would hold out. The smell was atrocious.

By this time, I suspected the campers were taking photos. It's a good thing this happened before social media, or I might have become a YouTube sensation, right behind the piano-playing cat.

Next, I heard the sound of objects striking the side of the outhouse, but it didn't sound like the goat was butting the door with his horns. It sounded more like hail pelting the outhouse, but that couldn't be. The sky was clear blue. I eventually figured out that the campers were trying to scare the goat away with pebbles, but most of their stones were hitting the outhouse.

When things quieted down, I opened the door once again. And once again I had to slam it shut before the goat could send me hurtling backward.

It felt as if the creature had me cornered in the outhouse all day, but I think it was more like 20 minutes. Every minute in an outhouse feels like an hour, so it's safe to say I spent the equivalent of 20 hours in there. Time truly is relative when you're stuck in such a purgatory.

After 20 minutes dragged by, I checked again and saw that the three goats were finally wandering away. The goat's two friends were probably telling him, "Man, you're a rock star! You *owned* that camp host!"

I sheepishly (or goatishly) slipped from the outhouse and retrieved my jacket, which lay on the ground, and I saw that one of the goats had defecated on it. Like I said, I get no respect.

I also didn't get much respect from the campers, who enjoyed every minute of my predicament. One man had been sitting in his chair and sipping coffee the entire time, and he said, "You were trapped in there so long that I finished one pot of coffee and was about to start another!"

Rob had joined the spectators, and he enjoyed himself thoroughly. I vowed that I would never again allow an animal to trap me in an outhouse. And it was a vow that I kept...for almost six weeks. I blame my diet for my second run-in with ornery wildlife (and my second run into the outhouse). This time we were floating camp hosts at Eklutna Lake Campground, and I was on a special water-torture diet in which I had to drink a couple of gallons of liquid to "wash away" the extra pounds. One inconvenient result was the constant urge to visit the nearest facility.

However, one of the outhouses at the Eklutna Lake site had a serious problem. The previous camp host had cordoned it off using yellow caution tape—kind of like the tape you see at crime scenes. He had warned us that this outhouse was off-limits because the tree above it held a nesting goshawk. And anyone who knows anything about goshawks understands that they can be fierce when it comes to protecting their nests.

Female goshawks are actually a bit bigger than the males, with a body about 25 inches long and a wingspan of 40 inches. On the Alaska Department of Fish and Game website, this is what experts say about the northern goshawk: "The area immediately surrounding the nest is vigorously defended against intruders—the adults scream and dive at interlopers, slashing and grabbing at the offenders with their feet."

However, at the time I was not aware of any of this information.

I told myself, *It's just a bird. How bad could it be? It's not like it's a pterodactyl!*

Besides, I had to go to the bathroom *really* bad, and this was the only outhouse at the campsite within a reasonable distance. The next closest one was 20 campsites away, all uphill. When I glanced up at the tree, I saw no sign of movement in the nest, so I figured that the mother goshawk had flown the coop for the time being. If I moved fast enough, I could get in and out of that outhouse faster than you could say, "Here we go again."

Wrong.

Stepping over the caution tape, I rushed for the outhouse. I'm not sure where that mother goshawk was hiding, but I never reached the door in time. The big bird swooped down at me, talons outstretched, and struck my head—although with my cap and thick head of red hair, it didn't get down to my scalp and draw blood.

Screaming like a baby (I mean, yelling loudly in a very manly way), I covered my head with my arms as the bird came down for a second dive-bomb attack. This time it jabbed me in the arm, and then it came around for a third swoop. I swung wildly at the bird, and the goshawk actually took off my Alaska State Parks ball cap, dropping it to the ground. What was it about these wild animals and their lack of respect for the symbols of my camp-host authority? As the goshawk wheeled around for another attack, I found safety in...you guessed it...the outhouse.

How in the world could this happen to me again?

Panting and perspiring and gagging on the odor, I could hear the goshawk screeching. She was probably perched on top of the tree, just waiting for me to emerge. With the mountain goat, I was able to wait him out and finally escape, but this situation was completely different. The bird's nest was directly overhead, so I would not be able to wait her out. She was going nowhere, and I was trapped.

I had my trusty state park jacket once again (washed of the goat droppings), so I decided to cover my head with it as I made a run for safety. There was no use waiting around inside this outhouse, so I threw open the door and rushed out, my coat completely covering my head, like a criminal trying to hide his face from the paparazzi as he is hurried into a waiting squad car.

I heard the goshawk scream.

If I had thought this through, I might have realized a major limitation with making a mad dash with a coat over my head: I could not see the branch on the ground. I tripped and went flying facedown onto the dirt. Goshawks evidently do not know the rule, "Never hit a man when he's down," because the bird hit me again and again, swooping and swooping and swooping at me.

With my jacket still over my head, I tried to crawl to safety like an infantry soldier squirming beneath a tangle of barbed wire. But in my case, the barbs were the sharp talons of the goshawk, and she kept striking me on the back, leg, and arm. This wasn't working. As I scrambled to my feet, a roar rose up from the gallery of campers who had gathered to watch.

"Run! Run!"

So I did. I took off running, and the mad bird continued to dive-bomb me before finally deciding that I no longer posed a threat.

Once again, I had attracted a crowd—although fortunately Rob hadn't been there to see my second humiliation. I didn't plan on telling him what had happened, but the story spread like wildfire, and I never heard the end of it. One of the campers even wrote me a letter, addressed from the goshawk, telling me she was sorry for attacking me and hoped she didn't ruffle my feathers—or some nonsense like that.

The ribbing was so bad that I eventually had to string some of that caution tape in front of the door of our camper. I warned that I was going to attack (goshawk style) the next person who crossed that tape and teased me about what had happened.

But you know, I deserved the teasing. After all, if I had to put one word to my encounter with the goshawk, it would be "hypocrisy." I had been clearly warned about the goshawk and had even warned others, instructing them to stay away from the outhouse. But I went ahead and ignored the warning when it suited me. This is exactly how we behave when we apply Scripture to others but not to ourselves. What a perfect picture of hypocrisy.

As anyone who has ever read the Gospels knows, Jesus has some harsh words for hypocrites, who were usually Pharisees trying to trap Him. He lashes out in Matthew 23:2-4.

> The teachers of the law and the Pharisees sit in Moses' seat. So you must be careful to do everything they tell you. But do not do what they do, for they do not practice what they preach. They tie up heavy, cumbersome loads and put them on other people's shoulders, but they themselves are not willing to lift a finger to move them.

This is hypocrisy at its worst. You place burdens on others and expect them to live up to certain standards, but you do not live by the same rules. We detest politicians who pass laws and then find ways to exempt themselves from those same laws. So why do we do it in our own lives?

The image that Jesus uses is perfect. He talks about putting heavy loads on other people while we walk along jauntily, not lifting a finger to help. In the ancient world, there actually was a position known as "the burden bearer." That was their job—carrying heavy loads on their backs, held in place with very strong rope. If a burden ever became too heavy, the burden bearer could ask a passerby to help hold up the load for a moment so he could rest. Enlisting the aid of someone else was much easier than putting down the heavy load and then lifting it up again. In the same way, we are called to share each other's burdens.

We display our hypocrisy in all kinds of ways, but it usually comes back to the same principle. We expect others to carry a heavy load we are not willing to carry. We expect them to live by rules we do not follow. We expect them to stay behind the caution tape, but we do not expect ourselves to do it.

But when we cross that line, we do so at our own peril because hypocrisy can come back to bite us. Come to think of it, hypocrisy can also head-butt us or swoop down on us. And if we're not careful, it might even snatch away our dignity, along with our Alaska State Parks hat.

7

MY FORTRESS OF MULTITUDE

I woke up freezing because it was a December day, and winter in Alaska is not for the faint of heart, especially when you live in a tiny tin can of a camper with little heat. I slept wearing gloves, a hat, and a heavy coat because the only heat in our camper came from a small electric heater and the propane stove, which I couldn't use too much if I wanted to continue my lifelong habit of breathing.

When I woke up, I could see my breath, which was nothing out of the ordinary. We could *always* see our breath inside the camper because it was perpetually cold. At night during the winter, it could get down to single digits, so it was like living in a metal ice cube tray. I kept an ice scraper handy at all times because as my breath condensed, it formed sheets of ice on the interior of the camper windows.

Rob's job had sent him flying off to Barrow, Alaska, so Sam and I and a cat named Rusty were all alone in the camper when I awoke on this cold morning. But when I went to exit the camper door, I discovered it wouldn't open. I shoved a little bit harder, but still nothing.

That was odd, so I threw my shoulder against the door. It was like I was hurling myself against a brick wall.

Scraping away some ice from the window, I peered out and discovered that I hadn't been running up against a brick wall. I had been butting up against a *snow* wall. Three feet of snow had fallen overnight, and it buried the bottom half of the camper. Opening the door was impossible.

I'm going to die, I thought. I was stuck in this freezing camper with no way out. I envisioned myself being discovered thousands of years from now, frozen in a solid block of ice—an ancient man preserved in his prehistoric Carhartts.

But I didn't become desperate until I smoked my last cigarette. Yes, I am sorry to say that at this point I had yet to give up the nasty habit, so when I stubbed out the last of my cigarettes, I felt doubly doomed. It's one thing to freeze to death, trapped in a camper; it's another thing to do so without tobacco. It occurred to me that I had another pack of cigarettes out in the truck, so my craving for smokes motivated me to escape from the cold camper. (In that sense, I suppose I can say cigarettes saved my life.)

Scraping away the ice from the inside of the window, I looked out and could see the truck, so close and yet so far. Determined to get to those cigarettes, I went to work on the largest window, eventually finding a way to yank it out. Next came the considerable chore of squeezing my body through the opening, kind of like squeezing toothpaste out of a tube—only I didn't flow out quite as easily. It was more like trying to squeeze that last little bit of toothpaste from the tube, and it just won't come out no matter how much you pinch it. However, I finally managed the impossible and squirmed out of the opening, doing a slow-motion dive headfirst into the bank of snow that buried our camper.

After all that, the only thing I could think was, *I need a cigarette*.

Thus began another ordinary winter day in Alaska.

As you may have noticed, I mentioned that we now had a cat

living with us. This new addition to our fold came about when Rob and I visited a farm feed store and decided to pick out a cat from a new litter of kittens—a squirming mass of orange fur inside a box. We stood by the box and prayed with great specificity: "Father, whatever cat you want us to have, let him jump out of the box. Then we'll know it's the right cat."

The moment we finished the prayer, I lifted the lid of the box, and instantly one of the orange kittens sprang out and leaped right into Rob's arms. Rob made a quick inspection of the kitten and put it back because the cat was a girl, and he wanted a boy.

"Hold on," I said. "Our prayer was for the first one that jumped out—not the first boy."

Just then, the same cat sprang out of the box, attached itself to Rob's shirt, and began to climb up his chest.

Rob shrugged and said, "Whatever."

He knew he couldn't argue with such a clear answer to prayer, so we brought the kitten home and named her Sheba. It wasn't until Rob was in the camper lying down with the kitten on his chest that I noticed something quite curious.

"Uh, Rob...I think Sheba's got a little surprise for you."

"Oh?"

"Take a closer look."

Rob did, and he immediately realized what I was talking about. Sheba was not a "she." He was a boy.

"It's a miracle!" I exclaimed, although I was pretty sure he had been a boy from day one. We named him Rusty, and he stayed a Rusty for the rest our time together.

Rusty, Sam, Rob, and I were now staying at the Eagle River Campground because the Briggs Bridge day-use facility had closed for the year. Eagle River was open for a few more weeks, so the ranger told us we could move there, making it possible to continue attending King's Way. The drive to church was only a few miles longer, but it could be challenging on wintery, slippery days.

Our church was wonderful to us. Realizing that we weren't exactly dining in style, a congregation member who worked for the Wonder Bread company regularly dropped off bread and milk. In addition, the water in the campground bathroom was frozen at this time of year, so James the Janitor let us use the showers in the basement of the church before he opened the building for the day. We were just getting by to say the least.

Meanwhile, Christmas was fast approaching, and I was feeling down in the dumps because I had no family in Alaska and no money to pay for a trip home to Washington State. Christmas had always been a major deal in our house when I was growing up, and my parents went all out. Every Christmas, their log cabin was decked out in decorations and packed with happy people, so Christmas brought up bright memories. But this Christmas was likely to be pretty dark and dismal because I was stuck in my frozen Fortress of Solitude. Superman's famous headquarters, the Fortress of Solitude, is sometimes depicted as being in the middle of an arctic wasteland, but at least he had light—and heat vision to keep him warm. At this time of the year, it was dark for much of the Alaskan day. The shortest day, December 21, saw about five and a half hours of light, with the sun rising at 10:14 a.m. and setting at 3:42 p.m.

Bottom line: It was depressing.

Fortunately, we had joined one of the church's home study groups. Pat and Sylvia McGuire, the same couple whose canoe Rob had rescued, were the leaders. And as Christmas approached, Pat and Sylvia invited the group out to their home. I will never forget walking up to the house and seeing at least two dozen Scandinavian ice candles, with flames flickering from inside hollowed-out circular blocks of ice. The ice candles were placed all along the sidewalk leading to the brightly lit house. It was magical, like something out of Disney's *Frozen*.

Pat McGuire was a higher-up with an oil company, so their house was magnificent. I entered through the foyer, which overflowed with winter boots. I still didn't own a good pair of boots, if you can believe it. So I yanked off my soggy old tennis shoes and placed them next to a long line of wonderfully warm boots. My tennis shoes looked pitiful, like a beat-up VW Beetle in a parking lot of Cadillacs. I vowed I would get myself a nice pair of boots of my own. Soon.

I then noticed that my right sock had a tiny hole near the toe, and I kept pulling on the end of the sock and tucking it under my toes, hoping no one would notice. This didn't help any with my normal awkwardness in new social situations. Gripping the end of my sock with my curled-over toes, I limped into the living room, and the sight of their decorations took my breath away in more ways than one. The house was so warm and toasty that I could no longer see my breath the way I could outdoors or in my camper. But it also took my breath away with its awe-inspiring beauty. The main living area rose up two floors and was topped by a cathedral ceiling. And in the center of the living room was the largest Christmas tree I had ever seen. It stood almost 14 feet tall, shooting all the way up to the second-floor balcony.

The youngest McGuire child, Shannon, was all smiles as she took Rob and me upstairs for a tour, and I said in amazement, "Look! The tree reaches all the way up here!"

"Yeah, I know!" Shannon said, grinning widely. "Cool, huh?"

"Verrrry cool."

Then we went downstairs for hot chocolate, and I saw at least 30 coffee cups hanging on display—each of them from a different place around the world where the family had visited. We had only three coffee cups in our camper—one for me, one for Rob, and one for Sam. I am well aware that dogs cannot drink from coffee mugs, but I had come across this mug with the name Sam on it at a garage sale, and I couldn't resist. Whenever Rob reached for Sam's mug, I would remind him with a stern look and firm voice, "That's Sam's."

"Whatever," he would say, slowly pulling his hand back and looking at me as if all this snowy desolation had finally unhinged my mind.

After coveting the McGuire coffee cups in their kitchen, I found a seat in the living room. I was probably being quieter and more observant than normal because with my attention deficit disorder, I was afraid of saying something socially goofy, especially in such a fantastic setting. So I just sat there quietly, taking it all in as I continued to play with the hole in my sock. Off to one side was a large harp, which I assumed was just a decoration—until Sylvia sat down and began to play. In fact, Shannon brought out her harp as well, and the mother and daughter played together. I had never heard a harp played live before, and I have only one word to describe it—ethereal. I felt as if I had stepped into heaven. Either that or I had wandered into a Norman Rockwell painting, or I was inside a winter wonderland snow globe.

Looking around the room, I saw that most of the people had their eyes closed as they savored the harp music, so I closed my eyes and prayed a very specific prayer. I asked that God would one day give me a beautiful house with a big Christmas tree and lots of friends who would rock the rafters with laughter. As a PS, I asked God if I could also have a kitchen like the McGuires', stocked with a multitude of coffee cups, which had come to symbolize hospitality and warmth to me.

We enjoyed an amazing evening, but as we drove home and trudged into our cold little camper, I had to admit to a touch of envy. I was back in our cramped, 21-foot tin can, thumping my arms against my side and trying to stay warm while I waited for the stove to pump a little heat into the place. I was miserable, so I started praying about my plight—whining, actually. (Is there such a thing as sacred whining?) And then it dawned on me. I looked out the window of our camper and realized that God had given us close to 495,000 acres of beautiful Alaskan wilderness, and it was all ours during the winter, when the campers were gone from Eagle River Campground and the expansive Chugach State Park.

The moon shone on the fresh snow, and I recalled the nights when we could see the northern lights shimmering in the sky. God had hung those lights in the sky just for us—with their greens and reds and blues. The Christmas decorations that God provided rose higher than any Christmas tree on earth, and I sensed more than ever that God was in control. I may have been living in a metal camper, but I was in a camper in God's hands (although I wouldn't have minded if He had been wearing some warm mittens as He held us).

All evening, I had been feeling a bit like Job, though my trials were nothing compared to his. But the Lord had answered me by showing me His wonders—just as He had done with Job. God answered Job's complaints with words that ring true for anyone from Alaska. He spoke all about His creation.

"Have you entered the storehouses of the snow?" (Job 38:22).

"Can you bring forth the constellations in their seasons or lead out the Bear with its cubs?" (38:32).

"Do you know when the mountain goats give birth? Do you watch when the doe bears her fawn?" (39:1).

"Does the eagle soar at your command and build its nest on high? It dwells on a cliff and stays there at night; a rocky crag is its stronghold" (39:27-28).

Its stronghold. Those words hit me squarely between the eyes. God is my rocky crag, my stronghold. As Psalm 18:2 says, "The Lord is my rock, my fortress and my deliverer; my God is my rock, in whom I take refuge, my shield and the horn of my salvation, my stronghold."

When I turned away from the window of my camper, my eyes came to rest on the small, glowing Christmas tree sitting on our table—a light that my mother had sent to me as an early Christmas gift. My mom and grandma had made the light by putting crystal beads on safety pins, stringing them together in the shape of a tree, and then coiling Christmas lights inside. This was a wonderful symbol of how God creates beauty in our lives by stringing together the most ordinary moments, like shaping a beautiful Christmas tree out of ordinary safety pins and beads. Everything connects. Viewed on their own, safety pins and moments from our lives might seem plain, but assembled together by the Master's hand, they become stunning.

This little light of mine kept my camper from feeling more dismal than it was. To this day, it's still the first decoration I put out each Christmas when I start decorating for the holidays in September (the same month my mother sent me this Christmas tree light). I always put this light in a place of prominence to remind me of God's faithfulness and how He answered the prayer I said at the McGuire house. Today, I live in a house with a big kitchen, lots of mugs, three guest rooms, three flushing toilets, and not an outhouse in sight.

Next to the light, I always place a picture frame made out of rocks that my parents collected during their many gold-mining trips. (That's another story.) The rocky picture frame holds a photo of my old Alaskan camper to remind me that Jesus is my rock and my deliverer, even in the coldest and darkest of places.

Superman can keep his Fortress of Solitude. I have the greatest fortress of all—the Holy God of Israel. He is my Fortress of *Multitude* because He holds all of His creation, including a multitude of angels, in His protective embrace. On this special Christmas, I learned that God cares and He is aware. I learned that He wants to take us from our trailer in the wilderness and bring us into His mansion, where I am quite certain there will be warmth and light and a cup with your name on it.

And oh yes...plenty of harps too.

Before I leave the subject of Christmas, I have to tell you about my family's tree-decorating tradition back in Washington State—a story that goes a long way toward explaining why Christmas is such a special time for me. It also might explain some of my eccentric ways.

Every Christmas, my parents made a point of inviting to our house guys from church who served in the military but couldn't make it home for the holidays. My mother would tell them all about the heirloom ornaments that filled our huge Christmas tree. Some of the ornaments were handmade, some of them were quite expensive, and others were just tree fillers. But there was one ornament far more important than any of the others.

This ornament was my Grandma Burmaster.

I don't mean that the ornament used to belong to my Grandma Burmaster. I mean that the ornament was indeed my grandma.

My grandma was kind of odd (any surprise there?), and she said that when she passed away she wanted her body cremated and her ashes blown into four glass Christmas ornaments. That way, she could be given to each of her four children and hang around on their trees and celebrate Christmas with them every year. My grandmother came up with the idea after a friend gave her a Christmas bulb that had been hand-blown from the volcanic ash of Mount Saint Helens in Washington State.

I must confess that it always seemed singularly strange to think of my grandma as a Christmas bulb. In fact, no one in my family liked the idea of taking her out of the box, much less handling her. That's why we always extended the "honor" of placing Grandma on the tree to the soldiers who visited us on Christmas day. Some of them weren't very comfortable with the idea, but in the end they would all agree to do it.

When Rob came to our house for Christmas for the first time, he was given this rare honor. At the time, Rob was a petty officer in the Navy, so he was conditioned to be steely under pressure. The military had prepared Rob for almost anything—except handling Grandma the Christmas Ornament.

He agreed to do the job, but I could tell it made him nervous. So Rob went to pick my grandma's bulb out of the box, and very, very carefully he lifted it in the air. Then he slowly turned toward the tree, looking as if he were handling a live bomb. I could almost see the sweat beading on his forehead as he took his first tentative steps toward our tree.

That's when the worst happened.

Somehow, some way, the hook on the ornament, which is used to hang the bulb on the tree, popped loose. Gravity took over, and the bulb plunged toward the floor. Everything seemed to move in slow motion as Rob fumbled for the bulb, trying to catch my fragile grandma. His eyes went wide, his mouth opened in fright, and his hands grasped at thin air.

But the inevitable happened. Grandma the Ornament crashed against the wooden floor and splintered into a hundred pieces.

My entire family went quiet. Rob just stared at the floor in horror. Then he looked over at us, saw our expressions of silent shock, and gazed back down at my shattered grandma.

My grandmother was gone, broken to pieces.

All the blood drained from Rob's face as he bent down and began to sweep up the pieces with the edge of his hand.

"I'm so sorry…so sorry….so sorry…" he stammered.

I had to feel bad for the guy. Here he was at a Christmas party full of people he had never met, and he had broken their beloved matriarch. Still on his knees and sputtering apologies, he desperately wondered if Grandma could be pieced back together like some sort of Humpty Dumpty.

He was so panic-stricken that I don't even think he heard the doorbell. I bent down to help Rob collect the pieces of my grandma and said I would take care of it if he wouldn't mind answering the door. My mom came into the room with the broom and dustpan while Rob got up and went to the door, his face still beet red with embarrassment.

Rob opened the door and saw a short, sweet-looking old lady standing on the stoop, and she had a gauze bandage wrapped around her head. That was a little odd.

"You must be Robert," the old lady said, piercing him with her eyes. She shot out her hand to shake. "I'm Grandma Burmaster."

Rob took her hand, very confused.

"You're Grandma Burmaster?"

"You heard me, and I'm a little ticked that you dropped me right on my head. Don't they teach you to be more careful in the military?"

"What?"

"I mean, what if I had asked to be cremated and turned into a grenade or something?"

That's when we all broke out laughing, and Rob realized he had been the victim of our annual practical joke. My dad explained to him that he bought a new hand-blown glass ornament every year, and the hook on the end was fixed to release when it was lifted out of the box. My grandma was alive and well and having the time of her life. Every year, she stood at the end of our driveway, waiting for the signal that she had been dropped.

I realize this practical joke might seem a bit mean, but these soldiers are tough, and they all survive. Besides, it was my grandma's idea, and she lived for pulling this Christmas prank each year.

This was Rob's first introduction to me and my bizarre family, and to his credit he didn't run for the hills. We became the best of friends, and in a strange way that practical joke makes me appreciate family and friends and grandmothers all the more.

This Christmas tradition reminds me that our relationships are fragile and must be treated with large doses of love and compassion. Unfortunately, it isn't always that way because tensions among family and friends can run high, especially around Christmastime, when the hectic pace of the season drives people to say and do things they regret. That's why counselors do a bustling business around the holidays. (The retailers aren't the only ones who thrive.)

I'm not saying that when we're with family, we should walk on eggshells, afraid of what we might say or do. I'm simply saying we need to treat our family with the same kind of tenderness as someone carrying a hand-blown, heirloom ornament.

Christmas is about love of family and love of friends. So as you approach any big family event with trepidation, remember the immortal words of 1 Corinthians 13:4-7.

> Love is patient, love is kind. It does not envy, it does not boast, it is not proud. It does not dishonor others, it is not self-seeking, it is not easily angered, it keeps no record of wrongs. Love does not delight in evil but rejoices with

> the truth. It always protects, always trusts, always hopes, always perseveres.

These words are God's guidebook to loving relationships and probably should be posted prominently at all family events. Study the words carefully, and this Christmas give your grandmother a big hug—but not so hard that you break her.

9
CABIN VERTIGO

I could not believe I found myself in this predicament once again! I woke up trapped.

In a previous story, I was trapped by three feet of snow blocking the door to the camper, but now it was even worse. I woke up *frozen to the floor*.

This time I couldn't blame the snow or our tiny camper. Rob and I had just moved into a compact cabin, which was owned by a kind hearted ranger. She was concerned about our well-being in our icebox camper and told us we could live in the cabin free of charge. What a blessing! This was our very first night in the cabin, and we didn't have beds, so we put our sleeping bags directly on the floor, figuring the carpet would give us cushioning and warmth.

Big mistake.

The cabin was located in the middle of a wetland protection area, so it was raised three feet off the ground, resting on top of railroad ties. This allowed cold wind to come whistling beneath the cabin, turning the floor into an ice rink. The layer of condensation created between the sleeping bag and the carpet turned into a layer of ice. We probably would have been better off using a Zamboni instead of a vacuum cleaner to clean the floor.

The upshot was that when I woke up, my sleeping bag was frozen solid to the floor. As if that wasn't bad enough, I couldn't move my arms, and I was trapped, mummy-like, in my ziplock freezer bag. Squirming like an overweight caterpillar in a too-tight cocoon, I slowly worked one arm free. But when I finally got my right arm out of the bag, I discovered that my sleeping bag's zipper was also frozen, encased in ice, and I couldn't get out.

Rob soon woke up to the sound of me calling his name—loudly and repeatedly.

"Rob? Rob...ROB!"

He was stretched out on the opposite side of the room, huddled close to the wall, but his sleeping bag had also frozen to the floor. His zipper was frozen as well, but having a less substantial physique, he had a little more room with which to work and was able to wiggle his way out of his bag. He then helped extricate me from my bag, and we proceeded to pry our sleeping bags loose from the floor, yanking up the carpet that they had become frozen to overnight.

As cold as it was in the cabin, I was thrilled to be out of the camper and into a larger space—the only structure in sight on 80 acres of land. But if cabins had personalities, I would say this place was slightly deranged. Jesus warned people not to build their homes on sand because it didn't make a solid foundation, but He might have said the same thing about building a cabin on a wetland. Because the cabin rested on railroad ties, and because the railroad ties were sinking at different rates into the muck below, the floor of the cabin was anything but level.

When you entered the only door leading into the house, you walked uphill into the kitchen. But the moment you exited the kitchen door and moved into the living room, you were suddenly going downhill. Take a right into an adjoining room, and you were going downhill in a different direction. Gravity pulled this cabin north, south, east, and west. Even the stairs leading to the tiny second floor didn't know which way was which. Gravity yanked them backward and sideways, so walking up those stairs was like climbing the Leaning Tower of Pisa. If you were upstairs and the phone rang downstairs, getting down those crooked stairs and scurrying downhill through the living room made you feel like a dizzy sailor sliding down a tottering mast in a storm and then rushing across a slanting deck.

We named our new home Cabin Vertigo, and when I put up the sign on the front door, saying, "Welcome to Cabin Vertigo," I made sure it hung crookedly.

To top it off, when you exited the cabin, you had to watch out because only three feet away, positioned directly in front of the door, was a tree that shot up through the deck like a ship's mast. (There's that nautical theme again—very fitting for a cabin that was sinking.) I ran into the tree face-first several times before tacking a warning sign on the bark at eye level that simply said TREE and had an arrow pointing straight up the side of the trunk.

Before we moved into the cabin, some New Zealand campers had been occupying the space for a spell, and they left behind all their decorations—if seaweed, barnacles, and an old fishing net qualified as decorations. The ocean had seemingly barfed in our living room. The house was also jammed with garbage of all kinds, which couldn't be blamed on the New Zealanders. Debris had simply built up after years of no one using the cabin. I spent two full days clearing it all out and hauling the trash to Anchorage.

Then there was the bathroom situation. Being in the middle of nowhere, we had an Incinolet composting toilet, which burned up the contents and sent smelly smoke into the air. On the hillside, not too far from where we lived, was a neighborhood of extremely wealthy homeowners who had a dramatic view of Mount McKinley (now known as Mount Denali)—although their view was periodically spoiled by billows of odoriferous smoke rising up from our tiny cabin. In fact, when I met one of the rich ladies from this hillside, the first thing she said was, "Are you the people with that burning toilet?"

Putting a more positive spin on it, I tried to think of it as a toilet and potpourri in one. Very pungent potpourri. Once a week, we emptied the ashes in our garden, and you should have seen our cabbages. They were huge! Of course, we didn't eat them, but we did use them to make homemade sauerkraut as a Christmas gift for relatives we didn't like.

Being poorer than church mice, we made do in this crazy cabin. We found the backseat of an old Volkswagen Beetle and used that as our couch, although the seat rose only about five inches from the floor, and we had to sit with our knees almost in our faces. Our only kitchen table was made out of cardboard and had a massive hole in one corner. It looked as if it had been clawed by an angry bear with no table manners.

One Sunday morning, I set my Bible on the table as I reached for my coat. The Bible suddenly vanished, as if the table had swallowed it in one big gulp. The Good Book had tumbled through the hole and smacked against the floor.

"All right, that's it!" I said. "Let's pray!"

Right then and there, I launched into a prayer about our furniture situation: "Father God, I ask You to keep us safe on the road to church and keep our hearts and hopes on You and PLEASE GIVE US A TABLE! I'm not asking for the cattle on a thousand hills—just one table with four legs."

When the Israelites wandered around the wilderness for 40 years, wondering why their GPS couldn't pick up a signal, they complained an awful lot. They had a difficult time trusting that God would provide, even after all the miracles He had performed in Egypt. "They spoke against God; they said, 'Can God really spread a table in the wilderness?'" (Psalm 78:19).

We too were in the wilderness, and so we tried our best to trust and believe that God could spread a table for us in our Alaskan cabin—a table without a gaping hole.

Our prayer was not lengthy—just simple and direct. Then we headed out the door.

After church that day, our friend Teresa invited us over for coffee at her new place in Anchorage. We jumped at the invitation because we were always looking for any excuse to be out of our cold cabin and into someone else's warm home. Teresa may have been offering us coffee, but we were even more interested in a heaping serving of heat.

Teresa was a wonderful woman whom we had met at the campground and helped lead to the Lord. A true granola, hippie spirit, she had spent several years traveling with the Grateful Dead and making the most creative, beautiful jewelry. Some of her jewelry was even sold at the Anchorage Museum. So there we were, the three of us sipping coffee and thanking God for the warmth, when there came a knock on the door. Teresa answered it, and she found the man from the upstairs apartment standing on the threshold and grinning.

"Hey! Anybody here need a table?" he announced.

I nearly choked on my coffee.

"*We* need a table!" I shouted.

"Then check it out," he said, leading us upstairs where his gift awaited.

The man explained that he was moving and had to be out of his apartment that very day. Goodwill and Salvation Army were closed on Sunday, so he needed to get rid of some final items—including a table. It was a beautiful little table, an amazing answer to prayer. How often do people show up asking if anyone wants a table, only a few hours after you pray for one?

Feeling pleased as punch, we loaded the table in the van and headed to Rob's work, where he had to take care of some odds and ends. Rob worked for a security firm, and as I stood around waiting for him to complete his tasks, a man from the business next door popped his head through the door.

"I'm getting ready to throw out a table," the man announced. "You guys need one?"

Rob stopped what he was doing and turned and stared. I too just stood there with my mouth open so wide, a 40-pound salmon could have jumped inside.

"You have *what*?" I asked.

"A table I'm getting rid of. You want it?"

We did. The table from Teresa's would be perfect in our main room, but we could use this second table upstairs to hold towels and such. Right now, the towels were stacked on the floor.

Shaking our heads in amazement, we loaded up yet another table in Rob's van and paid a visit to another good friend, Gillian. She had two huskies—the most insane dogs in all of Alaska, but she liked them that way. She regularly claimed she would never want a dog as obedient as Sam. "Dogs should be dogs," she would tell us. Huskies are not known for being obedient, as her dogs so aptly demonstrated. They're known for running aimlessly in any direction except the direction you want them to go.

Besides being a generous friend, Gillian was a wonderful baker, so she had asked us over for treats—and a second serving of heat. But before we could even walk inside her home, she greeted us at the door with the words, "I was hoping you guys would stop by. I've got a table I want to give you."

What in the world was going on? We ask God for a table, and He provides us with *three* tables in one afternoon! I had to check the sky just to make sure several more tables weren't about to rain down on us like manna from heaven. Gillian's table was a clever piece of furniture that attached to the wall and could fold down or be raised up when you needed to use it. It would go well as a small buffet table next to the kitchen table we received from Teresa's neighbor.

We added the third table to our growing collection, and our van looked like a furniture delivery vehicle.

Receiving those three tables in one day was nothing less than miraculous, but not all of our furnishings came to us that way, dropping out of nowhere. We often had to go hunting for furniture and other items. We discovered that the end of the month, when people's apartment leases were ending, was a good time to find discarded stuff. We were not too proud to dumpster dive, and we found all kinds of goodies, including a sack of computer memory that Rob sold for $120.

Why should we be too proud to dumpster dive when that's what God does all the time? He uses broken, used-up people to carry out His plans. Before I became a Christian, I assumed that God used only perfect people. I assumed that heroes like David were perfect because I had been aware of only the inspiring stories, like the time he killed the giant Goliath. When I learned the full story—his affair with Bathsheba and his arranged murder of her husband in battle—I saw just how flawed these heroes could be.

God is more than happy to use people whom others consider rubbish. He renews and redeems and repurposes people in the same way we repurposed the things we found for our cabin. I discovered that God could even use me—a D-plus student with ADHD and OCD. (That's a lot of D's. Evidently, if there's a D in a condition, it was mine.) To top it off, I was not popular, not athletic, and always offbeat. It's as if God went dumpster diving one morning, and when He looked into a trash bin, He shouted in delight, "Oh, lookee here! It's a Torry! Do you want to come out of this bin?"

"Oh yeah, You betcha!" I answered, and He lifted me up.

How could I not trust a God like that? In Alaska, I had seen His hand at work in so many ways and through so many people. He provided us with shelter, furnishings, and heat (although on many winter mornings, the glass of water near my bed was frozen solid). God also brought light into our lives. Our cabin had electricity, but we relied on lanterns for light until some good friends gave us our first real lamp—a hurricane lamp. This simple, solitary light might have even saved Rob's life.

One night we had been walloped by a blizzard, and Rob was coming home from work with a huge load of groceries. As usual, he piled all the groceries in the sled and prepared to drag it along the 200-yard trail leading back to our cabin. But the snow was coming down so hard that he was blinded and had no idea where the cabin was located. We had lights strung along the path, but for some reason they weren't working. We also put down boards and pallets on the trail because in the spring and summer the ground was mushy, but on this snowy night, all the boards were completely buried.

Without lights and guideposts, Rob strayed off the path and started going in the opposite direction from our cabin. He dragged 100 pounds of groceries on the sled, including a huge frozen turkey, and he trudged through incredibly deep snow, straining with every step. When the snow got up to his waist, he was certain something was wrong. He was pretty sure he was walking in the opposite direction, risking the possibility that he might become as frozen as the turkey he was lugging.

Who knows how long Rob would have been lost in the blizzard if he hadn't suddenly noticed a patch of snow in one direction that seemed just a little bit lighter than the other snow. He couldn't see any lights, but he could see a slight reflection on the snow. Rob realized that the faint light, barely visible, was the glow from our lone hurricane lamp. Wise men follow the light, so he worked his way back up a steep slope and eventually found the path to the cabin.

It's not always easy to trust that God will provide, especially on days when He doesn't seem to hear our prayers. When I feel as if God is not listening, my mind always goes back to those pivotal moments, such as when He set a table for us in the wilderness. God provided—not so much our wants, but our needs. Sometimes God's provision is truly miraculous, as it was when we received those three tables in one day, but sometimes His activity is not so obvious. Trusting God can be a lot like slogging your way through a blizzard, as Rob did on that cold, snowy night.

In the mad rush of daily life, seeing God's hand at work is about as easy as spotting a faint light in the middle of a blizzard. But when we do see the light, however faint, we should head in its direction. Trust the Source of that light. It's the only way to find your way home in a storm.

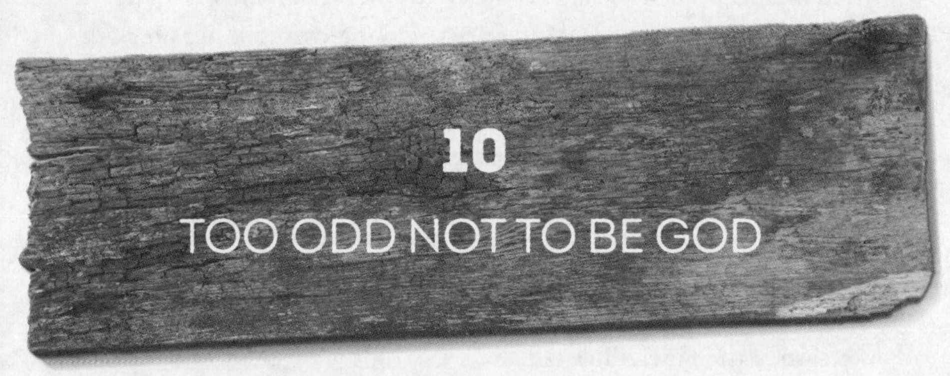

10

TOO ODD NOT TO BE GOD

My friend Haroldean ("Dean") Anderson was only eight years old when she heard an audible voice of God for the first time.

Dean vividly remembers standing in the foyer of her small church in Nebraska, listening to a missionary from Alaska drone on and on about his ministry on the Last Frontier. Nothing this missionary said about Alaska remotely interested the young girl.

That made it all the more shocking when Dean suddenly heard a voice. "Someday, you are going to Alaska."

Dean never told anyone about this experience at the time because how does an eight-year-old explain that God spoke to her? Nevertheless, she held this memory in her heart, and fifteen years later, Dean came to Alaska. I got to know her in a Bible study taught by our pastor's wife, Ann Aiken. As we worked through one of Kay Arthur's studies from Precept Ministries, I was amazed at Dean's intelligence and sensitivity to the Holy Spirit.

I am often skeptical of people who say, "God told me..." because some use it as a way to prevent others from challenging them. If God told them, how can you argue with that? But Dean is not one of those people. She is a woman of integrity, and God works in her life with power and authority. The fruits of her faith are plain to see.

Dean and her husband were the ones who gave Rob and me the first light in our cabin—the hurricane lamp that guided Rob back home in the blizzard. In the same way, their lives have served as a beacon, illuminating the hand of God in my own life. Even today, the story of how Dean came to Alaska and how her husband came to the Lord remains a light and an inspiration, so let me share a condensed version of their incredible tale.

By the time Dean was 23 years old, she was newly divorced, had a young daughter, and had fallen away from the Lord. But every once in a while, she still wondered if and when she would someday go to Alaska. That's when her best friend (also newly divorced) moved to the Last Frontier to be near family.

"Promise me you will move to Alaska too?" Dean's friend said to her before departing.

So this is how I go to Alaska, Dean realized.

Confident that Alaska was where she was destined to go, Dean purchased one-way tickets for herself and her daughter, and she immediately became smitten by the grandeur of the state. However, shortly after her friendship fizzled and her job went up in smoke, she was virtually penniless. She and her daughter moved into an apartment with two bags of groceries, their suitcases, and two foam pads on which to sleep. That was it.

"I was at the end of my rope," she says, "but I believe God's office is found at the end of your rope." So she knocked on His door and simply said, "God, You see my situation. You know I need a job, a new place to live, and transportation. Can You help me?"

Immediately, she says, "God began to woo me back with His kindness." She began to experience miracles, often in the nitty-gritty details of her life. As just one of many examples, she asked the Lord for a dresser because she and her daughter were storing their clothes in cardboard boxes in the apartment God had provided for them. Three days later, a friend told her he had just lost the lease on his storage unit, and he wondered if he could keep all his furniture in her apartment for an extended period. Just like that, her apartment was furnished—and not just with a dresser, but also with a beautiful table, chairs, beds, and end tables.

Furniture coming from out of nowhere…Now, where did I hear that before? As Dean put it, these things were "too odd not to be God."

About this time, she felt the Lord urging her to become involved in radio even though she knew absolutely zilch about it. She even felt drawn to challenge the local Christian radio station about their lack of music for young people in Anchorage.

And then it happened again. Dean heard an audible voice from God.

She was just getting into her car when God told her, "Start praying for Larry Wayne." Larry, she would later learn, was a popular rock-and-roll DJ in Anchorage. Dean decided that praying for Larry would certainly be a lot easier than challenging radio stations about their music selections.

"So I told God okay," Dean says, "even though I didn't know where Larry Wayne could be found on the radio dial."

For some odd reason, she also felt led to enter an essay contest sponsored by Larry's station. The winner would get to spend two hours on the air with him. Spending two hours live on the radio sounded terrifying, so her first reaction was, *Absolutely not!* But she couldn't shake the sense that God wanted her to enter this essay contest, and she reluctantly did.

Meanwhile, God kept giving strange signs to Dean. At a Sunday night service, a guest speaker from England approached her, saying he had a word for her. He proceeded to tell her things about her previous marriage that only Dean and God had known, and then he gave her an even more startling message. He told her the Lord was going to give her a husband within a year. Dean was stunned because she wasn't even dating at the time, and no one seemed to fit the bill.

A few days later, she awakened to an urging from the Lord, telling her, "Wake up and get dressed. Someone will be at your house in 20 minutes." Sure enough, about 20 minutes later a person from the radio station arrived at her apartment, telling her she had won the essay contest and would be the first person to appear with Larry Wayne on the two-hour show. (Dean still couldn't afford a phone, so the station had sent someone out to deliver the news in person.)

"I freaked out in front of the man from the radio station," Dean says. "I literally started pulling my hair and saying, 'No, no, no!'"

Startled, the man backed up a few steps, holding up his hands and assuring Dean that she didn't have to go on the radio if she didn't want to.

"But you don't understand," Dean said to him. "I *have* to do this."

Obediently, she went to the radio station, where she met Larry Wayne, the man the Lord had asked her to pray for. When Larry first saw Dean walk into the station, he thought, *Good-looking redhead. Maybe this contest won't be so bad after all.* But that's when Dean shot out her hand and declared, "Hi, I'm Dean. I'm a Christian."

Yikes.

Suddenly, Larry saw this contest going downhill faster than a waxed toboggan. Larry was recently divorced, and his life was a stream of partying, drinking, drugs, and chasing skirts. The last thing he needed was a Christian fanatic spending two hours on air talking about Jesus.

To Larry's surprise, the two-hour show went smoothly. Dean had a good personality, she was quick-witted and funny, and to Larry's great relief, she didn't talk about Jesus on the air. As they parted, Larry told her she had done a wonderful job and added, "Don't be a stranger." Dean thought that was the end of things.

She and Larry had no contact over the next month. Dean fasted for three days as she continued to pray for Larry, and she felt the Lord telling her to invite Larry over for dinner. She had no romantic interest in this foul-mouthed, loose-living disc jockey because he represented the very lifestyle she had recently left behind. Still, God's direction was clear, so she invited him to dinner.

When Larry entered the apartment and saw all the nice furniture (the stuff that had been loaned to her by the friend), he said, "Nice apartment."

"I have a good provider," Dean said, referring to God. But Larry wondered if she was talking about a sugar daddy.

The two of them spent nearly four hours at dinner, talking about God's plan for our lives—something Larry had never heard before even though he had gone to church as a child.

"I'm thinking...*really?*" Larry recalls.

At first, Larry could barely tolerate Dean because all her talk about Jesus wore him out. But as he got to know her better, she slowly transformed into a friend and then a best friend. Larry liked hanging out with Dean, but he wasn't interested in church. In fact, God told Dean, "Stop inviting him to church."

Dean couldn't invite him, but that didn't prevent a mutual friend of theirs, a man named K.B., from inviting Larry to a special church service sending K.B. off to start a new congregation in Milwaukee. Larry couldn't very well get out of this request, and at last he reluctantly agreed to go to their church.

Then came the turning point. A few days before the service, Larry woke up depressed after another hollow night of partying.

"I was in the shower, and I suddenly began to cry," he says. "I really wanted answers. I was tired of my life as it was. My life was a nothing existence. So in my tears, I said to God, 'If You're real, help me.' Little did I know that I had just opened the door for God. He's always a gentleman and never forces Himself on anyone."

A few days later, Larry finally set foot in Dean's church. This Anchorage church was large with two enormous wooden entry doors.

As Larry stepped through that doorway, he suddenly felt as if he were standing beneath a waterfall.

"I knew it wasn't a real shower, and it wasn't like the roof was leaking," he says. "But mentally I had a vision of me standing under a shower, and the water was cleansing me. What I had done in my past was gone."

He didn't tell Dean what happened to him in church that day, but she sensed immediately that something had changed. When the service ended, he said to her, "What time is church next Sunday? I'm coming to your house and picking you up, and we're going to go."

Dean's prayers had been answered.

The next two times Larry attended Dean's church, he experienced the same "waterfall" sensation when he passed through the main doors. Larry had been transformed, and so had his relationship with Dean.

He compares his initial relationship with Dean to two magnets on reverse poles, repelling each other. They were not attracted because the spiritual chasm between them was just too great. But when Larry turned his life around, he says, "It was like when you suddenly turn one of the magnets around, and BOOM, they come together. That's exactly what this relationship was like. I had turned around. My poles were being reversed."

Dean and Larry married one year and ten days after she had been told, "You will be married within a year."

Okay, so there were an extra ten days there, but who was going to quibble? By the time I met Dean and Larry at King's Way in Eagle River, they had been married for more than ten years, and their faith and their story were both challenging and inspiring. The biggest lesson I learned from them was that God cares about the small stuff—things like furniture, entering radio contests, praying for foul-mouthed, lost disc jockeys, and inviting someone to dinner or to church.

Some people say God doesn't bother with this kind of trivia. With wars and famine and disasters, He's got too much on His plate to care about furniture. But Dean and Larry showed me that if God could create the intricacies of every life form on earth, down to the smallest molecule, He certainly has the capacity to care about the tiniest elements of our lives. Jesus made this clear:

> Are not two sparrows sold for a penny? Yet not one of them will fall to the ground outside your Father's care. And even the very hairs of your head are all numbered. So don't be afraid; you are worth more than many sparrows (Matthew 10:29-31).

In the grand scheme of things, our lives are not "small stuff." Dean's choice to obey God, pray for Larry, and enter that contest changed both of their lives—and it changed millions of other lives. Dean and Larry went on to do a radio show together in Alaska that still continues to this day (although it's now hosted by someone else). Larry also became one of the four founders of Air1—a Christian radio network that today reaches about 8 million people across the United States. He now hosts a show on the K-LOVE radio network, which reaches 14 million souls.

All of this can be traced back to a simple sentence Dean heard God speak to her in a parking lot: "Pray for Larry Wayne."

C.S. Lewis famously said, "There are no *ordinary* people. You have never talked to a mere mortal. Nations, cultures, arts, civilizations—these are mortal, and their life is to ours as the life of a gnat. But it is immortals whom we joke with, work with, marry, snub, and exploit—immortal horrors or everlasting splendors."

With Lewis's kind permission, I would like to add to his quote. In addition to there being no ordinary mortals, there are no ordinary events in our lives. What we do during our mortal existence has eternal consequences. Our choices echo through eternity, so keep your eyes peeled for God's work in your life, no matter how small something seems.

Also...*listen.*

Not everyone hears the audible voice of God the way Dean has. The only time most of us heard a voice from above is when the hostess at Cracker Barrel announces over the PA system that our table is ready. But keep your spirit tuned for the voice of God, and you *can* hear Him speaking—even if it is not with audible words. Just as we sometimes have to fiddle with a radio dial to fight through all the static and get a clear signal, it can take effort to fine-tune our receivers to the will of God. But He's there, broadcasting every day to every heart.

11
DRIVING ME CRAZY

Forrest Gump famously said, "Life is like a box of chocolates. You never know what you're gonna get." The same could be said about buying a cheap, well-used Jeep from the post office.

Shortly after arriving in Alaska, Rob and I realized we were going to need to buy a second vehicle. Our other one was white, and I kept losing it in the snow. So I set about the business of car shopping. It was summer at the time, but I knew winter would be fast approaching, so I looked for something that could handle the snow and the mountains where we lived.

I made an exhaustive search for a new car, which in man-speak means I bought the first vehicle I saw. The post office in Anchorage was selling used Jeeps for $2000 apiece—not a bad deal—but the catch was that you couldn't test-drive them. You had to pick one out blindly and hope and pray that it held together without duct tape.

I wound up with a 1982 CJ8 Jeep, and through the summer it drove great, although I had to get used to driving on the wrong side. Post office Jeeps always have the steering wheel on the right side—the passenger seat in a normal car.

When the first snow arrived with winter, I discovered the Jeep's many limitations. The heater didn't work, the defroster was faulty, and the Jeep had removable doors, so it wasn't airtight—although why the post office would want removable doors on their Jeeps in an arctic climate is beyond me. What were they thinking? "It's freezing in here, but I still have feeling in my toes. Let's get rid of the doors and fully commit!"

So this was the vehicle I was soon driving around Alaska in freezing temperatures and on snow-packed roads. As Forrest said, you never know what you're gonna get, and metaphorically speaking, I had bitten into the most awful piece of chocolate in the box.

The only one who seemed satisfied with the Jeep in spite of its many flaws was Sam. I suspect this was largely because he liked to sit completely upright in what appeared to be the driver's seat, and he reveled in the looks of envy from other dogs as he appeared to drive by.

The defroster was on the blink, so I kept an ice scraper in the front seat. As I drove, I kept one hand on the steering wheel while I scraped the inside of the windshield. I would even lean over and clean Sam's side of the windshield because he too needed a clear view of the road, just in case he had to take the wheel in a pinch. (Sam would probably have been a better driver anyway.) I also kept a second ice scraper on hand. This one had a long handle that allowed me to open the window and reach out and scrape the *outside* of my windshield as I drove. While I was at it, I would use the scraper to whack the windshield wiper, which regularly froze in place.

The scary part was that I was a dubious driver even when I wasn't trying to scrape windows and steer at the same time. Ask Rob about my driving habits, and he'll probably mention the snowy day when I risked driving on the slick roads to the Walmart in Anchorage just so I could talk to one of the people greeters. I was that desperate for human contact.

I was about four miles down the road when I hit a patch of ice and lost control of the Jeep. Suddenly, I felt as if I were in the teacup ride at Disney World, spinning around and around and around and trying to turn into the spin, as they always say. When I slid off the road and into a snowbank, I had no choice but to call Rob at work.

"What was so important to get at Walmart that you had to drive out in the snow?" he said. "Whatever you needed I could have picked up on the way home."

"That might have been awkward. I needed a people greeter."

"What?"

"I need human contact with someone who didn't snap at me every time we talked—or say 'whatever' every other sentence."

"Whatever."

"The people greeter *has* to talk me," I explained. "It's his job. Besides, it's like free therapy. You should try it."

"A few more years with you and I'm sure I'll need counseling."

So Rob left work and drove out to rescue me, hooking the tow strap to his truck and pulling me back onto the road.

"Follow me into Anchorage, and I'll make sure you get there," Rob said with a scowl.

So I drove as carefully as possible, keeping my eyes focused on the back of Rob's truck. The road was snow-covered and slick, but I was doing fine...until I reached the Rabbit Creek overpass. I didn't realize at the time just how dangerous an icy overpass can be. Because an overpass doesn't have the ground beneath it—only air—it loses heat rapidly and freezes easily.

I learned this lesson the hard way when I reached the overpass. Suddenly, my Jeep was sliding sideways down the road, and I'm like, "Wooooaaaaahhhhh!"

I made it across the overpass, but on the other side, I ended up in a ditch once again.

Even worse, Rob hadn't been checking his rearview mirror regularly, and he was long gone. So I called him on my cell phone.

"Are you still behind me?" he asked.

"Technically, yes."

"What do you mean 'technically'?"

"Well, I'm behind you, but I'm in a ditch…again."

Rob was becoming technically ticked. But he wheeled around, drove back, hooked up the tow strap, and hauled me out of the ditch for a second time.

When we finally reached Walmart, safe and sound, he told me, "You better plan on spending all day with that greeter because I'm not going to tow you again. I'll stop by Walmart after work and follow you home."

"Fine," I said. "Five hours at Walmart. I can do that."

But five hours in a single store wasn't as easy as I thought, especially since the greeter turned out to be rather unsociable. He was friendly for a couple of minutes, and then I think he began to suspect I was trying to take his job.

"Hi, welcome to Walmart!" I exclaimed to the shoppers as they strolled into the store. "Do you want a shopping cart?"

I was just trying to be helpful.

When I finally gave up trying to become buddies with the greeter, I began wandering throughout the store. For three long hours.

I actually managed to entertain myself for a couple of hours before becoming bored out of my mind. You can spend only so much time alphabetizing the soup section. So, deciding I could not wait another two hours for Rob to get off work, I told myself I could drive home without an official escort. Good grief, I was a grown man! I could do it.

I barely made it out of the Walmart parking lot.

I was turning right out of the lot when my Jeep hit a patch of ice, and once again I was on a Disney World ride. This time I slid up and onto a six-inch-high concrete median separating the two lanes of traffic. I wound up perched on the median with my left tires hanging over one edge and my right tires hanging over the other edge.

None of my wheels were touching the ground, so I was stuck. Motorists honked, shaking their fists and gesturing wildly, as if to tell me, "Hey, you're on the median, mister!" As if I didn't know that! What, did they think I chose this as my parking spot?

I was so embarrassed that I ducked down really low when I called Rob on the cell phone so none of the passing motorists could see me. All they could see was our dog Sam sitting upright in the driver's seat. As I said, post office Jeeps have the driver's side and passenger's side reversed, so it looked as if Sam had driven up onto the median.

Sam just stared back at the people. *What're you looking at? You try driving without opposable thumbs! There was a cat—I swerved!*

With growing trepidation, I dialed the phone.

"Rob?"

"Yes?"

"I've got a problem."

"Let me guess. You left Walmart and you're stuck in a ditch somewhere."

"You're half right. I did leave Walmart, but I'm not in a ditch. I'm on a median."

"A what?"

"A median. You know, those are the things that separate the—"

"I know what they are."

I explained the situation to Rob, glad that I had the distance of a phone connection separating us. Grumbling, he agreed to drive out once again, and I waited in my Jeep, feeling growing embarrassment.

When Rob drove out to Walmart to tow me for a third time in one day, he was fuming. At first, he didn't say a word. Moving swiftly, he got out of his truck, staring daggers at me as he hooked the tow strap to the back of his truck and then to the front of my Jeep. Finally, he stomped over to the Jeep and knocked on the window.

Rolling down the window, I tried to lighten the mood. "Oh look, Sam, there's Rob! What a surprise!"

Rob was not amused.

"You're gonna want to hold on to something," he says.

So I held on to the dashboard as he towed my Jeep, and with a mighty BUMP we were pulled off the median. Then Rob, still hitting me with a laser-like glare, got out of his truck, unhooked the tow strap, and knocked on my window again.

This time, when I rolled down the window I didn't try to lighten the mood. Without a word, Rob handed me the tow strap.

"Here," he said. "Keep the tow strap. The next time you get stuck, you can wave down anybody you want. You're not calling me."

"That's not a very Christian attitude," I said. Probably not the wisest choice of words, but correcting my spiritual mentor always made me feel better. However, it just served to further annoy Rob. Apparently, I had pushed his missile launch button.

As Rob returned to his truck, he ran his hand along the vehicle's cab, gathering just enough snow to form a nice round snowball. Spinning around, he hurled the snowball at my Jeep, and it went *poof!* on the windshield just in front of my face.

He followed me home just to make sure I made it safely, and then he took away my keys for safekeeping.

On that day, I discovered that driving in Alaska was a good training ground for understanding the challenging words of Jesus: "Enter through the narrow gate. For wide is the gate and broad is the road that leads to destruction, and many enter through it. But small is the gate and narrow the road that leads to life, and only a few find it" (Matthew 7:13-14).

In my experience, the road is not just narrow. It's also icy and snow packed.

In Alaska, the snow falls so heavily that plows often settle for clearing just a single lane in one direction and a single lane in the other direction, creating a narrow path through the mountain of snow and requiring you to be constantly on your guard. Evidently, God's lane is just as narrow, and I often wonder, "Lord, why can't You give us a ten-lane highway that leads to life? Why does the wide road lead to destruction?"

But the reality is that God knows life is treacherous—like a narrow, icy road. Dangers are all around, and the precarious nature of life requires us to be vigilant. Therefore, like any good parent warning a child to drive carefully, God wants us to understand that if we race down this slick road, we will inevitably wind up in a ditch.

So stay on the straight and narrow and icy—and if you need someone to talk with, you don't have to shovel through six feet of snow and maneuver down icy roads just to spend time with a Walmart greeter, as nice as they are. God is right there, right now, ready to listen, and He never gets tired of towing us out of ditches.

12
DRIVING ME CRAZIER

The day I had to be towed three times was terrible, but it didn't hold a candle to one memorable Sunday.

Rob and I had a routine we followed religiously on Sundays, and it started with going to church, where most things that we follow religiously usually begin. After church, we would go to the Laundromat to wash clothes, then to the post office to pick up our mail, and finally to the grocery store. But this Sunday would be different. This Sunday Rob had the flu, which meant I had to do everything myself.

I hated doing my own laundry, much less his. But being a Christian and having a (GRIT MY TEETH) servant's heart, I loaded all the dirty clothes into the laundry bag and tossed it in the sled, along with Sam. Then I climbed on top of the laundry bag, and Sam and I coasted down the trail to the Jeep. The laundry's padding made the bumpy ride much easier, although the box of Tide could leave its share of bruises if you weren't careful where you placed it.

At the bottom of the path, I reached the Jeep and slung the huge sack of dirty laundry over my shoulders. I looked like jolly old Santa

Claus, except the dirty underwear and other items jammed into my sack would have made lousy gifts for some very disappointed children on Christmas morning.

When I reached the vehicle, I was disgruntled to discover that the lock on the driver's door had frozen solid. I had no idea that a locked door could freeze like that. Remember, I was from Los Angeles, where things like that just didn't happen. Door locks don't freeze in LA. They get hijacked along with your car, but they don't freeze.

Actually, I had no idea why I even bothered locking the Jeep in the first place. We lived in the middle of 80 acres covered with nine feet of snow, and the nearest neighbor was a mile away. No one was likely to hot-wire the Jeep and go for a joyride, although there was one moose in the area that had pretty shifty eyes.

I didn't ask Rob for help with the Jeep door, and I'd like to say it was because he was sick, but the truth was that I was more concerned about my pride. I felt too stupid to ask him for assistance. I tried to solve the problem myself, jiggling the handle and banging on the door with my elbow and fist and even my hips. That's when I came up with the idea of breathing hot air onto the lock, so I leaned down close to the lock, cupped my hands around the keyhole...and proceeded to freeze my top lip to the door.

Yes, I had acted out the famous scene from *Christmas Story*, only it was my lip, not my tongue, that had become affixed to the metal. I tried to gently pull away, but my lip stretched like silly putty. I also couldn't shout for help with my lip attached to the door and our cabin 200 yards away. I could see the headline in the *Anchorage Daily News*: "Man freezes lip to Jeep door and dies of subzero stupidity."

Finally, I yanked back a little harder and my lip snapped free, although a little piece of skin remained attached to the lock. Wincing from the sting, I went back to work on the lock. After about 20 frustrating minutes, it suddenly occurred to me to check the passenger door.

Walking around to the other side, I found that, sure enough, the passenger door was open, although why I locked the driver's door but not the passenger door was beyond me. Maybe I thought it'd be okay if someone broke in just so they could sit in the passenger seat and rifle through the glove compartment, but I'd better lock that driver's door so they can't get behind the steering wheel and drive off with my Jeep! Never in a million years could a thief figure out that all they had to do was scoot over.

Apparently, I'm not the type of guy who takes a bite out of crime. I just prefer to nibble on it.

With the passenger door open, I proceeded to climb in—not as easy as it sounds, especially with a huge sack of laundry and Sam. Also, I am a very large man, and this Jeep was a very small vehicle. To make matters worse, the front seats were bucket seats, and in between them was a deadly stick shift. I could see yet another headline: "Man impales himself on stick shift 20 minutes after freezing lip to door."

Once I climbed into the driver's seat, I leaned all the way over, grunting and straining as I hauled in our monstrous laundry bag, which held an entire week's worth of work clothes for two bachelors. Then I called Sam, and he bounded into the passenger's seat. Getting everything inside this small Jeep was as complicated as strapping an astronaut into a rocket. And before this day would end, I'd be saying the equivalent of "Houston, we have a problem" about a dozen times.

I proceeded to make my various stops, beginning with church, the Laundromat, and the post office. Each time, I had to go through the same tortuous process: lean over, open the passenger side door, let Sam out, push out the laundry bag, climb over the stick shift, scoot across the seat...and that was just getting out of the Jeep. I had to go through the whole process in reverse to get back in!

Suffice it to say I was soon in a very bad mood, especially when I went through all this rigmarole at the post office, only to discover that our PO box was filled with bills and not a single letter from home. Apparently, only my creditors loved me. I was so angry that I took it out on poor Sam.

"Out!" I yelled at Sam when I had stomped out of the post office and opened the door to the Jeep.

"In!" I shouted after I had climbed in and yanked the laundry bag back in behind me.

I think this was the precise moment when I fell out of fellowship with the Lord, if you know what I mean. In frustration, I made a last-ditch effort to open the driver's door, and I threw all of my considerable weight against the frozen door.

CRACK!

I blinked in amazement. Hallelujah—the door had opened!

I was just getting ready to sing "Victory in Jesus" when I realized that I had done more than open the driver's door. I had *broken* the door. To be exact, I had broken the tiny aluminum connector piece that keeps the door shut—the part that goes *click* when you shut the door. I was not a happy camper. I was now a frenetically crazed one. My door had gone from frozen shut to not being able to close at all.

My next destination was Walmart, and now I had to drive all the way there while holding the broken door with one hand and steering with the other, occasionally letting go of the door so I could scrape the inside of the window. I needed three hands, but somehow I managed to make it to Walmart without driving off the road.

But now I faced a whole new problem. Because the driver's side door didn't shut, there was nothing to stop Sam from nudging open the free-swinging door and jumping out while I did my shopping. So I hauled my laundry bag out of the Jeep and jammed the bag against the outside of the door to keep it closed. But that raised yet another problem. What if someone came walking along and spotted my bag of freshly washed laundry just sitting in the parking lot and decided to make off with all our clothes? As a crime deterrent, I carefully reached into the laundry bag and grabbed all my neatly folded, supersized, 3XL underwear and placed them directly on top of the bag. If this didn't discourage a would-be criminal from stealing my laundry, nothing would!

After finishing my shopping, I was just getting set to leave Walmart, still frustrated with a door that wouldn't close, when I was struck with a brilliant idea. I remembered I still had the tow strap in the backseat—the one Rob had given to me after he had to tow me out of the snow three times in one day. I realized I didn't have to keep holding the broken door with my hand while driving if I used the tow strap to tie the door to the steering wheel.

Basking in my brilliance, I tied one end of the tow strap to the door and the other end to the steering wheel. Then I attempted to back up...and discovered that because the strap had no slack I could no longer turn the steering wheel.

Panicking, I tried to yank the steering wheel to the right and to the left, but it wouldn't budge. It was fixed in place by the stupid tow strap! (Note that I'm calling the strap stupid, not the person who tied it.) I tried to brake, but the wheels hit a patch of ice, the Jeep began to slide, and I was unable to stop until I slid directly into a lamppost. After untying my strap from the steering wheel, I got out to inspect the damage, and I saw that I had put a nice V-shaped dent in the Jeep. My idea had not even been smart, let alone brilliant.

I felt like kicking the vehicle, but the way this day was going, if I tried something like that, the Jeep would probably fall completely to pieces. I climbed back inside, my mind racing. There had to be *something* I could do to keep the door closed before I took off for my final stop—the grocery store. If I couldn't tie the tow strap to my steering wheel, perhaps I could tie it to *my waist.* Yes, that's right. One end would be tied to the Jeep door and the other end would be tied to my waist.

Once I had the strap secured around my waist, I took off for Carrs grocery store to pick up two essentials that I couldn't find at Walmart—amazing whole-bean coffee and Moose Tracks ice cream. These two things would keep me going for an entire week. Incredibly, Alaskans' consumption of ice cream is the highest in the country per capita, and I did my part to keep them at the top of the rankings.

Alaskans assume that if it's freezing outside, they might as well freeze their insides too.

It was a little tricky driving with the strap tied around my waist because I had to lean to the left so the strap would remain taut and keep the door shut. If I sat up straight, the strap would go slack, and the door would pop open.

But to my utter amazement, it worked, and I managed to make it to the grocery store even though I appeared to be leaning over and talking into Sam's ear the entire way.

It wasn't until I was getting out of the Jeep at the grocery store that trouble struck yet again. I opened my door and began to step out of the Jeep, intending to untie the strap from around my waist. Talking to myself, I just happened to use the word "okay."

Saying the word "okay" was not okay.

This was our "release word" for Sam. We had trained him well—he would obediently sit for us until we released him with the word "okay." As soon as he heard me speak that word, he bolted. Sam decided he'd had enough of being cooped up in the Jeep on this crazy day, so he shot from the passenger seat and bounded over me, out the driver's door, and into the busy parking lot.

I went nuts—terrified that Sam would get hit by a car in the parking lot. So I reacted on pure instinct. That's my only excuse for what happened next. I took a couple of steps, intending to pursue Sam and rescue him. There was one tiny problem. I still had one end of the tow strap tied around my waist and the other end tied to the door. Everything seemed to be moving in slow motion as I felt the yank of the strap, slid on the ice, and fell backward on the ground. At the same time, the strap pulled on the door, causing it to slam directly into my face as I tried to sit up.

WHAM!

I was living in a cartoon.

Sam came back on his own, concerned for his master, but he felt completely useless because he didn't know how to apply a Band-Aid, untie a strap, or call 911. All I was thinking was, *Where's Lassie when you need her?*

Fortunately, a woman had witnessed the entire incident, and she approached and offered her assistance. I sat on the wet ground, stunned and bleeding profusely from a cut in my forehead. The woman's eyes went from me to the strap to the door, back to me and the strap, and finally to my forehead.

"Ooh...I think you're going to need stitches," she said.

"Actually, I don't think so. This strap around my waist is working quite nicely as a tourniquet, thanks."

The woman didn't laugh.

I was only partially joking about the strap becoming a tourniquet. When it yanked me off my feet, the knot around my waist had become so incredibly tight that neither one of us could get it undone. So the poor woman had to go into the grocery store and find a checkout clerk with a box knife to come outside and cut me free from my door. I can only imagine how that conversation went.

"Uh, excuse me...there's a man in the parking lot who has tied himself to his Jeep door and is bleeding badly. I think it's some horrible suicide attempt gone awry."

It took a while for the guy to slice through the heavy-duty tow strap with the box knife. As he cut away, no one said a thing. Not a word. I just stood there, holding a rag to my head to stop the bleeding and feeling like a complete fool. Meanwhile, the woman didn't leave. She just silently watched the employee cut the strap, probably thinking to herself, *I'm going to stand here until this thing is done because this is going to be the best story the bridge club has ever heard.*

Finally I was free, so to lighten the mood I quipped, "That'll teach me to miss a therapy appointment."

"Yeah, you really need to keep every one of those appointments," the lady said in a serious tone before wandering away.

After the bleeding was under control, I decided I might as well do my grocery shopping. But I noticed that as I pushed my cart around the store, I kept attracting stares from everybody. Fat people are used to getting stares, especially in places where there is food, such as restaurants or grocery stores. I can always notice when people cast sly glances into my cart to check out how much food a person needs to eat to get my size.

In the cereal aisle, one person just wouldn't stop staring at me, so I finally turned to him and said, "*What?* You've never seen a fat person before?"

The person stared back at me, mouth open in shock. Then the little kid turned and went running back down the aisle to tell his mother on me.

That's when I suddenly realized what all the staring was really about. I noticed that I still had the tow strap tied around my waist, and it was dangling behind me like a nylon tail. I must have looked like some overweight Jethro who had wandered down from the mountains to buy his cereal.

It was the final humiliation in a day chock-full of them.

When I finally got home, I was too embarrassed to tell Rob what had happened, so I planned on keeping the story to myself. But as soon as I walked in, Rob took one look at me and asked, "What happened to your head?"

"Nothing."

That's all I said. It was time to change the subject. But Rob asked again, only this time he used my name so I would know he was serious.

"TORRY...what happened to your head?"

I just shrugged. "I bumped it."

Rob still wasn't satisfied with my answer, so he did the thing I hate. He talked down to me and spoke his words slowly and clearly, and he even mimed his words with hand motions, as if I was too stupid to understand English.

"Torry. What. Happened. To. Your. HEAD!"

Everybody knows that when people talk down to you, the best

way to put them in their place is to raise your voice a little and talk down to *them*. That way, they get the message that they're the stupid one, not you. So I added my own mime actions for good measure.

"Rob. The. Jeep. Door. Was. FROZEN!"

Rob studied me for a second before responding.

"So you tried to head-butt it open?"

That comment really lit my fire. I immediately launched into the story, recounting every gory detail—freezing my lip to the door, breaking the door, denting the Jeep, tying the strap around my waist, the scene in the parking lot, the employee with the box cutter, the embarrassment in the store...With every sentence, he kept laughing harder and I kept getting angrier.

"It's not funny!"

When he finally brought his laughter under control, he said, "Why didn't you just come and ask me for help in the first place? I would have given you my can of lock de-icer."

"Lock de-icer? What's that?"

Rob walked calmly to the coatrack, reached into his coat pocket, and pulled out a tiny can. "Lock de-icer. Locks freeze in subzero temperatures whether you lock them or not. That's why everybody carries these in their pockets. All you do is spray it into the keyhole."

"Can I cook with that stuff? I've got a couple of steaks that need defrosting."

He rolled his eyes. "Also, why didn't you just come in and ask me for help? You know I'm a mechanic."

"I was afraid if I told you, I'd look stupid."

He paused. "Oh, I get it. Well, how do you feel now that you told me you tied yourself to your door?"

I had to ponder that for a few seconds before I replied. "Stupid?"

We all do dumb things that we're afraid to admit, either to friends or to God. But by being afraid to admit our shortcomings, we lock ourselves out of so much that God has for us. He wants to help us *before* we make matters worse. He wants to open the doors in our lives—the doors that we have allowed to freeze shut. But we're often too proud to confess our mistakes and too ashamed to ask for help. So we just keep on scraping and driving and scraping some more, and we eventually end up tying ourselves to things we have no business tying ourselves to until we start hitting our heads against the door of life and leaving ourselves bloody and banged up with far more to be embarrassed about than we ever did in the first place.

Psalm 107:13-14 says, "They cried to the LORD in their trouble, and he saved them from their distress. He brought them out of darkness, the utter darkness, and broke away their chains."

There it is, spelled out in black and white. Whenever you get stuck, call out to God, because He is like that patient and understanding best friend sitting up in the cabin just waiting for us to come in and ask Him for help. We'd be wiser if we did that in the beginning of our trouble because by the end of our journey, we no longer have just the original confession to make—that little fender bender. Now we're bringing the Lord an almost totaled car. But the good news is that Jesus is not like most insurance companies. He won't do the repairs and then cancel your policy, saying you're costing Him too much money. He's already paid a lifetime premium for us, so we can go to Him and ask for forgiveness—day after day—no matter how stupid our actions may be.

God is your doctor when you hit your head, your mechanic when you break down, your lawyer when you need defending, and the best friend you could ever have. So when you reach the end of your rope, or your tow strap, call out to Him, and let Him free you.

One other thing. Let God do the steering. He's a much better driver, especially when you're on thin ice.

13
OF MOOSE AND MEN

Early one morning, I had just trudged into the kitchen in search of coffee when I couldn't help but notice a full-grown moose wandering only a few feet from our window. And I mean this moose was huge! Males can get as big as 800 pounds and eat more than 60 pounds of food a day—a pretty hefty amount for a plant eater. How many vegetarians do you know who put away 60 pounds of leafy greens every day? That's a lot of trips to the salad bar.

I decided to help Mr. Moose in his pursuit of vegetation overload, so I tapped on the glass and slid our kitchen window open. After the Rudy the Reindeer incident, I had learned not to invite large mammals into my kitchen. I dangled a carrot in front of the moose's nose, and he gobbled it down, kindly preserving my fingers in the process. That was fun, so I rummaged around in the refrigerator and brought out a second carrot, which he gobbled up in short order.

I had lived in Alaska long enough to know that moose are perhaps the most dangerous mammals in all of Alaska—responsible for more injuries than even bears. People generally assume that moose, being slow moving (except when they're charging at you), are as lovably dense as Bullwinkle of cartoon fame. They don't give the animal the respect it deserves.

For example, I heard about a cross-country skier who didn't give a moose any respect—or distance. While skiing along a path near the University of Alaska, this fellow came upon a moose blocking his way, so he reached out with his ski pole and poked the moose from behind. The moose wheeled around and trampled him to death.

You may have heard the expression, "Don't poke a bear." Apparently, that applies to moose too.

In another case that made Alaska news, a moose stepped over a lady's backyard fence in search of food. Although moose are massive, they have long, spindly legs, so this guy could easily step over her fence. The lady, realizing that her little dog was out in the backyard with an uninvited moose, rushed out to save her pet—and was trampled to death.

Rob and I had already learned firsthand how touchy a moose can get, especially a female protecting her young. On an entirely different morning at the cabin, I walked by the large picture window in our living room and thought, *Is that a moose and her newborn calves?*

I moved closer to the glass and peered out. Yes, that definitely was a female moose, and she had just given birth to twins! It made for a heartwarming scene. The calves were incredibly cute as they struggled to rise up on their wobbly legs. They looked around in wonderment and nuzzled their mother, who was probably saying to them, "It's okay, this is the world. We own it."

The mother moose was only about six feet from our cabin, between our burn barrel and the picture window. Moose often give birth to twins, although one of the pair inevitably doesn't make it through the first winter. For the next two days, the mother remained close to our house with her two calves because she didn't want to journey far until her babies were strong enough. As a result, we were stuck in our cabin. Seriously.

Whenever Rob or I opened the door to the cabin, mama moose

went on high alert. She stared in our direction and began snorting a warning. She would lower her head, and her ears would flatten back, a sure sign that she was preparing to do a tap dance on our backs. Each time, we would quickly retreat into our cabin. The mother moose was telling us, "My twins are right here, so you're staying in there. Don't even think about leaving." A mother moose looks at everyone as someone who might potentially want to eat one of her babies. One look at me, and she was probably thinking, *That guy is going to eat both of them.*

Moose have sharp teeth, but you have to be especially wary of their legs. They can kick with both their rear and front legs, and they can even kick to the side with them, which may explain why moose are considered the Chuck Norris of the animal kingdom.

So we weren't going anywhere. For two whole days!

Finally, on the third day—a good biblical number—mother moose left the scene with her two calves in tow, and we could get on with our lives.

My only other direct encounter with a moose came on a snowy afternoon when I was returning from the grocery store with bags of food. We kept our 200-yard path to the cabin passable by packing the snow down on a daily basis. When Rob left for work in the morning, he would load all his tools on a sled and pull it down the path, packing down the trail in the process. That way, we always maintained a sled's-width trail through the snow from our cabin to our car.

On this particular day, I discovered that a male moose had stumbled across our trail and probably thought, *Oh look! Some friendly moose friends have created this path just for me!* I spotted the moose blocking my path when I was about 30 feet from the animal. Because our path was barely the width of my sled, which was loaded with groceries, I was stuck between a moose and a hard place. To retreat to my Jeep, I would have had to step over the length of my sled, which would have been a challenge. The snow was too deep on both sides of the trail to go around the sled.

My other option was to find a way to get the moose to leave. Folks in Alaska often carry bottle rockets in their pocket just for this type of situation. You wouldn't dare shoot a bottle rocket directly at a moose, but you could shoot it near the animal to scare it off. On this day, however, I did not have any rockets in my pockets, so I suppose I was not being completely sane when I decided to toss my canned goods in the animal's direction. I wasn't going to throw the canned goods directly at the moose—that would be a sure way to end my life. I thought I would toss them to the side of the moose so he might see them in his peripheral vision and think, *Oh my, it's raining canned goods. I should leave.*

Moose are easily fooled. With a brain the size of a grapefruit, they're not the smartest animals on earth. I don't know if you have ever tried talking to a grapefruit, but if you have, you know they're not too bright.

Of course, I shouldn't talk. Considering some of the things I had done in Alaska, most moose in my area were probably telling each other, "Don't worry about the guy with the crazy hair. He has a brain the size of a peach pit."

The moose on our path busily nibbled from a nearby tree. (The word "moose" comes from an Algonquin word that means "twig eater.") So I hurled my can of tomato sauce, and it disappeared into the snow a little to his right. Oblivious, the moose just kept on eating, so I tossed my can of tomato paste in his direction. Still no success. Then I tossed my can of tomatoes, and the moose just continued to nibble. By this time, he was probably beginning to think I was the dinner entertainment. This was the moose equivalent of eating while watching TV, and I was his comedy show.

Eventually, after I had used up all of my ammunition except my box of pasta, the moose ambled away, clearing my path. But there was still a problem. When I started hurling my groceries, I assumed I could retrieve everything once the moose was gone. I hadn't considered the six feet of snow on either side of the trail. I had just lost all my groceries in the six-foot drifts and wouldn't see them again until the snow melted in spring.

That night we had buttered noodles for dinner.

One other thing about moose in Alaska. In this neck of the woods, they top deer for the infamous honor of being the most common large animal to be hit by cars. And the way that moose are built, they are even more hazardous to strike than a deer. Their legs are like four skinny stilts, and when a car slams into them, the legs break and the bulk of the animal—all 700 or 800 pounds of it—goes crashing through the windshield. It's particularly dangerous with low-slung cars, so you don't want to be in a Prius when you hit a moose. The gas mileage isn't nearly as good when you're driving with a 700-pound animal in your lap.

In Alaska, "moose versus car" accidents are so common that there is even a spot for "moose hits" on insurance forms. The state keeps a tally of moose hits and flashes the number on roadway signs just to remind drivers to keep an eye out for them.

But back to the moose at my kitchen window.

As I was saying, I was well aware of the danger posed by a moose, but I figured I was well protected by my kitchen wall. This moose wasn't about to climb through my window—not like the polar bear that had done just that in a snow cabin up north. When the polar bear stuck its head through one of the windows, the man renting the cabin slapped the polar bear in the snout! In retaliation, the polar bear squeezed through the window and killed the man.

So if you're going to take away any lessons from this chapter, here they are. (1) Don't poke a moose. (2) Don't slap a polar bear. But I was about to learn a third lesson: Don't let a moose stick its head through your kitchen window.

After I had given the moose a second carrot, I went back to the refrigerator to get a whole bag of carrots, and he stuck one antler through the window to find out where I was coming up with all this delicious food. I decided I had to get a picture of this animal because no one in the Lower 48 states would believe it. I went to the back room to get my camera, but by the time I returned to the kitchen, the moose had stuck his second antler through the window, and now his entire head was inside our kitchen. I remember thinking his antlers might make a handy rack for my dishtowels.

But then I made a big mistake. I went to pet his nose.

I didn't realize at the time just how sensitive a moose nose could be. I have since heard that a wolf can sometimes immobilize a moose by biting it on the nose. It's that painful.

I had no intention of biting his nose, but just the idea of petting him upset the creature. He yanked his head back, and his antlers slammed against the window frame. This freaked out the moose even more, and he went completely berserk, trying to retract his head from our window. But in his panic, he couldn't get his antlers through the opening. I attempted to help him out. I grabbed hold of his antlers and tried to steer them back through the window, but he was snorting and thrashing his head back and forth wildly and nearly threw me off my feet. (By the way, the antlers felt kind of soft. They call it antler velvet.)

Next, the window glass shattered, which did nothing for this poor moose's frazzled nerves. For a moment, I thought he was going to take down the entire wall, and then I really would have been in trouble. I would have shown up in the newspaper as another cautionary tale about not respecting the power of the moose.

Then I heard a resounding CRACK, and the moose pulled out the entire window frame. I stared in wonderment as the beast ran off into the woods with the window frame still draped over his antlers. I wonder to this day whether he started a new antler fashion trend among moose.

I was alive but shaken, and I had some serious 'splainin' to do when Rob got back and wondered why we had such a draft coming through our kitchen window.

When I look back on that day and think about the moose poking his huge head through our window and tearing the frame to pieces, it strikes me as a vivid picture of what sin can do if you give it even the slightest foothold in your life. Sin can seem innocent enough at first, like feeding carrots to a moose on a beautiful winter's day, but once it gets its nose and antlers into your house, look out!

The incident brought to mind Genesis 4:7, where God says to Cain, "If you do not do what is right, sin is crouching at your door; it desires to have you, but you must rule over it." The phrase that leaped out at me was "sin is crouching at your door." It occurred to me that when we are tempted to let unhealthy passions take control of our lives, sin is loitering right outside our door, just waiting for us to let it inside. Or in the case of my moose analogy, sin is right outside our window, waiting to shove its nose inside. Sin will use any entry point—a window or a door. The devil isn't choosy about the way he enters your house.

The devil may not have horns as wide as moose antlers (he probably doesn't have horns at all), but he can still wreak havoc if you give him the slightest foothold in your life. As the famed evangelist Billy Sunday once said, "Temptation is the devil looking through the keyhole. Yielding is opening the door and inviting him in."

In the passage from Genesis, God also tells Cain to "rule over" sin—a phrase that brings to mind our long history of finding ways to "rule over" wild animals. Today, most people in the Lower 48 have so little contact with wilderness and wild animals that they underestimate the dangers. Some people even look back with disdain at our ancestors' desire to rule over the wild kingdom, as if modern people would act any differently if they had to face wolves, bears, and other threats on a daily basis.

I see the same attitude with the devil. Just as urbanized people cannot comprehend the dangers of the wild, twenty-first-century people do not always comprehend the dangers posed by Satan. Belief in a personal, living force of evil is less common today, and as a result people underestimate his potential to wreak havoc in their lives. If people think about the devil at all, they think of him as a mythical being—a tame creature, not a "roaring lion looking for someone to devour" (1 Peter 5:8). People think they can poke the devil with a ski pole, and they don't see the danger until he wheels around and tramples them.

So don't give sin a foothold—or even a hoof hold. If you do, the devil might just tear down your entire house, not just the window frame. And while you're at it, please don't slap any polar bears. They tend to slap back—with claws.

14
THE BEAR REMOVAL TEAM

Sam scented a bear outside. We could tell by the way he was behaving. He was switched on, and his barks were coming fast and furious. He didn't take a breath between barks, and he lost complete control of his saliva, dog-spit flying in every direction.

If we could translate his barks into human speech, I'm sure he would be shouting, "THERE'S A BEAR THERE'S A BEAR THERE'S A BEAR THERE'S A BEAR THERE'S A BEAR!"

It was about four a.m. when Sam exploded into a nonstop barking frenzy, and in the Alaskan summer, that means it was just getting light outside. Rob and I both woke up to Sam's outburst, and Rob went straight for his pistol—a .22 caliber Ruger. Then he nudged open the door to the cabin, and there it was—the black bear we had seen in the vicinity on about six occasions. The bear was only about seven feet from our door.

We waited for it to move along, but as time ticked by, this bad-news bear wouldn't budge. The creature blocked the trail leading down to our vehicles, which was going to pose a problem for both

Rob and me if this she-bear didn't clear out. Rob had to take a work-related flight in a matter of hours, so he needed to get down the trail to his van. And I needed to take a flight later in the day for one of the most important professional events of my life—the Christian Artists Seminar in the Rockies near Estes Park, Colorado. I was scheduled to compete in the acting division of the seminar, which also featured contests in music, writing, and singing.

Rob decided to put a fright into the bear, so he aimed at the ground, not far from the large creature, and shot at least ten times. The dirt kicked up, and the bear finally moved—but it came right on back. It lumbered around the small belt of trees directly in front of our cabin, winding up back at our door.

"Shotgun," Rob said, handing me his pistol.

I was like a nurse at surgery, handing scalpels to the physician. Once again, Dr. Rob took aim at the ground directly in front of the black bear and fired away with his shotgun, kicking up another spray of dirt. The bear backed up a couple of feet, but that was as far as it went.

This bear was not afraid of anything, and a bear that has lost its fear of humans (and guns) is a very dangerous bear. We later learned that this same bear had been rummaging in the trash outside of a nearby house, trapping two boys in their garage for a couple of hours. This bear was clearly a menace to both people and pets—although in Alaska, folks are usually smart enough to never leave a dog outside. Dogs tied outside often attract bears, which gobble up all the dog food and then drag the pet off into the bushes for dessert.

We continued to wait out the bear, but it was not going anywhere. There was no way I was going to be able to leave the cabin, suitcase in hand, and simply say, "Excuse me, Mrs. Bear, I'm late for my flight, but if you'll just move to one side, I promise to share my bag of in-flight peanuts with you."

I had to admit, however, that part of me didn't mind missing my flight to Colorado because the idea of performing at the Seminar in the Rockies was about as scary as facing this bear. Our church secretary, Janie Downing, suggested I go to the Seminar in the Rockies because that's where a lot of people in the Christian entertainment industry first get noticed. I had been an actor in California before coming to Alaska, but this would be my first acting stint in a long time, other than a few performances at church.

Leading up to this event, I had written a sketch and performed it at our church, and then our pastor, Jack Aiken, did something he didn't do routinely. He took a special offering to raise money to send me to the Seminar in the Rockies. So how could I not go to Colorado and perform if my entire church was behind me? I *had* to go, despite my fears—assuming I could get past this bear. And this was no small teddy bear. Whenever I measure the size of things, I use a general rule: If I'm ever standing close to something and I feel svelte in comparison, odds are that it is BIG. This mama bear was about 250 pounds.

Rob didn't have a bear tag, so he couldn't shoot the bear legally. He called Alaska Fish and Game and told them the situation, hoping they would send out a bear removal team to trap the bear and transport it to a safe location away from people. However, the agency said we lived so far away that they couldn't get a team out to us for several hours. Rob needed to get to his plane soon, so he asked if he had permission to shoot the bear since it was clearly aggressive. They told us to wait it out, and if the creature didn't go away by the time Rob had to leave, he had the green light to shoot.

So we waited…and waited…and that bear simply would not leave. The bear was so stubbornly determined to stick around that I was beginning to think the Church of Latter Day Saints had sent it to our door.

Finally, Rob could wait no longer. By this time, the black bear was only a few feet from our cabin. Rob positioned himself on the threshold of the front door while I moved back and held on to Sam to keep him from attacking the animal. As the bear turned its head, showing its profile, Rob leaned a little to his left, took aim, and shot the bear right behind the ear. There was a risk that if he didn't kill the bear instantly, it might turn on us, claws ready. But it would be difficult for any creature to remain standing when someone fires a shotgun from such close range.

The big bruin hit the ground.

It appeared that the bear was dead, but we had to make sure. So I put Sam in a bedroom, and we went to investigate the results—very carefully. This sent Sam into even greater spasms of barking. Sam was our protector, and he went ballistic at the idea of us being outside with the bear but *without him*.

When we were finally sure the bear was dead, we opened the door, and Sam came tearing out at full speed. BARKBARKBARKBARK-BARKBARKBARKBARK! He was moving so fast that he ran right past the big mound of bear without even seeing it. "WHERE'S THE BEAR WHERE'S THE BEAR WHERE'S THE BEAR WHERE'S THE BEAR?"

Then he went tearing around the trees, sprinting in a half circle, and wound up back at the cabin's front door. At last, he looked down and finally spotted the big bear, sprawled out in front of our cabin steps. He went suddenly quiet and stared at the bear for about a second or two. Then it was back to what he did best—barking. "THERE'S THE BEAR THERE'S THE BEAR THERE'S THE BEAR THERE'S THE BEAR THERE'S THE BEAR!"

By this time, Rob was running late, so he left for the airport, putting me in charge of disposing of 250 pounds of bear. So I did what any normal person in Alaska would do when they have a bear on their doorstep. I called Alaska Fish and Game and asked them to bring in someone to cart away the carcass—a free food removal team, you might say. Without a hunting license, we were not allowed to keep the bear. The state would keep the hide and give the meat to the first name on a special list maintained by the state.

By about midmorning, a free food removal team drove out to

claim the meat—a real Alaskan meat and greet. Imagine my surprise when I saw that the group was comprised of a youth pastor and four teenagers. In the Lower 48, church youth groups play games and go to water parks. In Alaska, youth groups gut bears.

At first, the youth pastor began to do the gutting right there at the foot of our cabin stairs, but I was having none of that.

"I'm not going to have guts right in front of our cabin. You're going to have to take it down the trail."

So the youth pastor and the teens dragged the carcass halfway down the trail, chatting happily. "The backstrap of a berry-fed bear is much better than the backstrap of a fish-fed bear," the pastor said. (Try saying that eight times really fast.) The backstrap, by the way, is the best-tasting part of a bear.

"I'm really glad you guys live up here on the mountain," he continued. "That means this is a berry-fed bear, not a fish-fed bear. The backstrap of a fish-fed bear tastes fishy, but the backstrap of a berry-fed bear doesn't."

I think I followed all of that.

When the group found a good place to skin the animal, I left the youth pastor to his gory work, went back to the cabin, and finished packing. On the way to my Jeep, I had to step directly over the dead bear, luggage in tow.

Only in Alaska.

As I left for the airport, I assumed that the youth group would dump the bear guts in the woods, far from the path to our cabin. Little did I know that after the youth group had finished gutting the bear, they tossed the entrails just a few feet off our path. (Isn't there an old cowboy song about that? "Happy entrails to you, until we meet again...")

Thanks to the guts near our trail, when Rob returned from his short work trip, he was shocked to find a full-grown grizzly directly on the path. The creature had been lured there by the discarded guts and was having himself a jolly feast. This grizzly had to weigh close to 800 pounds, making the black bear look as small as a cuddly Star Wars Ewok.

Rob backtracked to his car and spent the next two days at a friend's house until it was safe to return to the cabin.

The crazy thing about this story is that about four years later, when I was no longer living in Alaska, I returned to the state to do my comedy routine, telling stories about the Last Frontier. I just happened to tell the tale of the black bear and the grizzly, and a man at the back of the room suddenly started waving his arms and announced that he was the youth pastor who had gutted that bear. After the show, he told me he was sorry about leaving the guts by the trail, but at least I got a good biblical message out of it.

That's right, I can even find a parable in bear guts.

In Matthew 12:43-45, Jesus says that when a man drives an evil spirit out of his life, it will try to return to the man, and it will bring seven other spirits more wicked than itself. "And the final condition of that man is worse than the first," Jesus said.

Those ugly guts are a lot like the evil spirit from Jesus's story—the spirit that had been driven from a certain man. When my youth pastor friend tossed those guts right by the trail, they attracted a grizzly that was far more dangerous than the original bear. The grizzly was like those seven spirits, which were far more wicked than the first spirit. After all, that grizzly was more than three times the size of the black bear.

In the previous chapter, the one about the moose poking its nose in the window, I talked about keeping evil out of your life. But there's another part to the lesson. When evil invades your life and you boot it out, make sure you get rid of it *completely*. When you drive a particular sin from your life—when you're disposing of the guts, so to speak—make sure you drive it far from you. If you don't completely clear the sin away, you're going to attract something far more insidious than the original sin. You're going to replace that 250-pound black bear in your life with an 800-pound grizzly.

Here's another important lesson to draw from Matthew 12. After you drive away a sin, replace it with God. In Matthew, note that when the evil spirit returned, it found the house "unoccupied, swept clean and put in order." Although the man got rid of the evil spirit, he didn't invite the Lord into his house to replace the diabolical lodger. The house, which symbolizes the man's life, was left unoccupied and abandoned. And we all know what can happen to an abandoned house. It becomes the perfect place for squatters. When you don't let God occupy your life, you become like an abandoned house, open for spiritual squatters.

So once you dispose of the "guts," make sure you invite God into your life, for He's the ideal lodger. He helps around the house and provides you with living water, and I hear He sets a nice table in the wilderness. By the way, this is by no means a lesson that I have mastered, and I have to remind myself of it daily.

After all that happened with the two bears, I am happy to report that Rob was eventually able to get back into our cabin, and I made it safely to the airport and flew to the Christian Artists Seminar in the Rockies.

There, things got even more interesting, but that's another story.

15
THE HIPPIE FOR THE HOLY ONE

I could not believe I was standing in the green room with the wildly popular singing group Point of Grace. There they were: four extremely attractive women and me (also extremely attractive but woefully underdressed in my Carhartt overalls). I was getting ready to perform at the Christian Artists Seminar in the Rockies, and I was about to be introduced by Point of Grace, a group that would go on to release five gold albums (more than 500,000 sold) and two platinum albums (more than one million sold). Who would have thought it possible?

However, being my usual awkward self, I had no idea what to say to these talented women. So of course I talked about our cabin's Incinolet composting toilet. What else was an awkward guy from Alaska going to chat about?

"That's really interesting," said one of the singers after I described the Incinolet toilet, which as you recall disposed of its contents by incinerating everything. "Come over here and tell the other girls."

Either she was really interested in Incinolet toilets and was planning to install one on their tour bus, or she simply could not believe that this was my idea of small talk. So she led me over to the other three women, and I repeated my riveting tale of the Incinolet toilet.

They smiled and nodded politely, but I was pretty sure they were not going to name their next album, "Songs of the Incinolet."

This pretty much summed up my first couple of days at Christian Artists—one awkward encounter after another. I suffer from severe social anxiety, so this conference was about as threatening as anything life could throw at me. Everyone at the seminar looked perfect and dressed immaculately, which brought back bad memories of the perfect church in Alaska that had exiled me to the balcony so I wouldn't accidentally show up on their television program. I felt like a fish out of water—like one of those salmon ghost fish, flopping around trying to breathe. I'm not blaming any of the performers, for they didn't ostracize me, but I still felt as if I were back in high school, eating alone in the cafeteria. It probably didn't help matters that I walked around the conference grounds in my Carhartt overalls. Several times, people asked me for directions, obviously assuming I was a custodian.

In addition to my social anxiety, I was terrified of acting at this conference because I hadn't performed for two years. When I came to Alaska and found my faith in Jesus, I decided I was going to spend two years away from acting, immersing myself in Scripture. I wanted to be grounded in the faith and to be serious about God, so I studied as many of Kay Arthur's Precept Ministries Bible studies as possible, and I listened to Christian programs, such as *The 700 Club* and Jack Hayford's broadcasts.

I cannot overestimate the impact of the Precept Bible studies on my life. I know this sounds like an old-fashioned, "I walked ten miles in a blizzard to go to school" story, but I really did walk several hours in the snow just to get to my Precept Bible study. I walked three hours to meet Rob at the highway by five o'clock so we could get to class by six. It was worth every step in the snow because these studies changed my life.

With all my attention on Bible study, I told my agent I was taking some time away from acting, but she had other ideas. Despite my protests, she kept setting up auditions for commercials and other gigs, and that's why I decided to grow my hair long. Let me explain...

As casting directors sift through pictures to decide which actors to call in to audition, they go strictly by your appearance in your photo. Therefore, when you show up for an audition, you had better look just like your eight-by-ten glossy. When I first came to Alaska, I had short hair and looked as fresh-faced as if I had just come from a Sunday school picnic—and that's how I looked in my eight-by-ten promo photos. So by growing out my hair, I no longer looked like my photos and essentially sabotaged any possible auditions, freeing myself up to study the Bible.

But Christian Artists was going to mark my return to acting, and my nerves were jangling. Nevertheless, I made it through the two early rounds of the conference competition. Imagine my shock when I learned I had been awarded the grand prize in the acting division. Unfortunately, winning the prize also meant I had to perform in front of a few thousand people, some of them the most popular Christian entertainers in the country. The audience even included some of my pastoral heroes, such as Jack Hayford.

I was petrified.

So that was how I found myself in the green room with Point of Grace, waiting to be introduced onstage. I made my entry from the back of the auditorium, and as I came forward (in my overalls, of course), I sang, "Papa G loves me, he loves me, he loves me!" I then faced the large audience and transformed the stage into Papa G's toyshop.

In my sketch, I also transformed myself into one of Papa G's treasured toys, a doll named Harry the Hippie for the Holy One. As Harry, I began by welcoming a new doll to the shop. Harry introduces himself and then tells the new doll a little bit about his life, hoping to make the visitor feel comfortable. Harry says that when he first came to the toyshop, he had a few problems, to put it mildly. He saw a lot of beautiful toys in the shop, and he noticed that he didn't look anything like them.

As I stared out into the audience of beautiful people, I realized that I too didn't look anything like them.

Harry then tells about his futile attempts to imitate the gifts of other dolls, including Singing Sarah, who sang like an angel, or Dancing Doris, who used her dancing to tell people about the Toymaker and his son, or Evelyn the Evangelist, who did cheers and got people excited about Papa G. Harry the Hippie for the Holy One says he even tried to imitate the Sam the Suit for the Savior doll, who was about as different from Harry as night was from day.

In the end, Harry says, he learned that each of Papa G's toys comes from its own unique mold, and that's the way the Toymaker likes it. But although none of the dolls look alike on the outside, we all share something in common—each of our hearts carries a special seal with Papa G's name on it. And nothing in the world can wipe off that seal except our own hand.

Harry goes on to explain that he finally learned his true gift, his true calling. His gift is nothing glorious, nothing flashy, and nothing that is going to get his face plastered on magazine covers. His calling is to stay right there in the toyshop, welcoming new dolls, being their friend, loving them, and praying for them when they go out into the world to tell everyone about the Toymaker and his Son.

This story resonated with my audience, which was filled with performers who do what most entertainers do—constantly compare themselves with the competition. But I was also speaking to myself through this performance. For so much of my life, I have suffered from Comparative Worthitis. I continually compared myself with others and never felt that I was good enough. As a result, I spent a lot of my life trying to squeeze myself into molds designed for others. One of the reasons I got into acting in the first place was that I felt more comfortable in someone else's skin. I felt better becoming another character than simply being who I was created to be. My life has been a long trail of discovering that I was never going to be Sam the Suit for the Savior or Singing Sarah or Dancing Doris or any of the others.

For better or for worse, I would be Harry the Hippie for the Holy One.

And then it struck me. When I walked down that long aisle at Christian Artists, I felt almost as if I was once again walking down the trail from my cabin when it was being blocked by a bear. To me, the audience at Christian Artists was that bear all over again. The performers and other Christian leaders in the audience were just as terrifying to me because they were the people I wanted so badly to love me. Thoughts of insecurity stood in my way. Would they accept me? Would they even like me? I wanted so much to be accepted, so stepping in front of that audience was like stepping over that bear, unsure whether it was going to rise up and tear me to pieces.

Ironically, this moment in my life became my Point of Grace. This was the point when I was confronted with the need to accept the grace that God gives me every moment of every day. I had to learn to give the same grace to myself.

By the time I finished my routine, the audience was on its feet, giving me a standing ovation—a great big bear hug, you might say. It was a surreal moment, and I felt as if I were riding a wave. I had found my true home among people who had accepted Harry the Hippie for the Holy One.

The problem was that once the thrill of the conference had worn off and I was back home in Alaska, I began to think it was all a fluke. I convinced myself that it had all been an act, and I had fooled everybody into thinking I had something valuable to offer. How could God use such a sinner as me? Before I came to Alaska and renewed my walk with God, I was highly skilled in the area of sin. In fact, if sin had a union, I would be the chapter president.

Then one day I was in the cabin watching a television evangelist, and he said something that was like a splash of cold water in the face. "Exercising our gifts is a matter of obedience," he said. "Failure to exercise our gifts can adversely affect the body of Christ and the very glory of God."

That woke me up. Evidently, ignoring my gifts was not an option. We are *all* called by God, and we don't have to wait for His audible voice before we get up and use our gifts. As Paul writes in Romans 12:6, "We have different gifts, according to the grace given to each of us."

Perhaps that's why God went out of His way to knock some sense into me and prove to me that I had something worthwhile to share with others. The very next year, I returned to the Christian Artists Seminar in the Rockies, which had changed its name to GMA Seminar in the Rockies. This time I entered the writing category, in which people could enter up to three sketches. I still thought the previous year's win was a fluke, so I prayed, "God, if You want to show me that You can use me, even with all my flaws, please let me place third." I wasn't asking for first or second, just third because I didn't know the difference between an adverb and a fraction, and I knew I didn't stand a chance against recognized writers.

When the results were announced, I was sitting way at the back of the auditorium because oversized folks like myself like to remain as inconspicuous as possible. I was stunned when Cam Floria, the president of the Seminar in the Rockies, announced the third-place winner, and I heard my name. Emotions hit me like a truck, and tears of thankfulness streamed down my cheeks as I made the long hike from the back row. The entire audience got a good look at this big, overly emotional guy, and I imagined that everyone was thinking, *Wow, the fat guy is really happy about third place*. It may have only been third, but it meant the world to me.

After accepting the award, I made my way back up the long aisle to my seat in the last row of the auditorium, only to hear Cam Floria announce my name as the winner of second place as well.

What? I didn't even ask for that! Are you kidding?

So once again, with tears in my eyes and feeling foolish and grateful all at once, I wheeled around and made my way back to the stage.

"And you might as well stay here," Floria said when I was on the stage. "You also won first place."

It was like a Sally Field moment, after she won her second Academy Award and famously said, "I can't deny the fact that you like me! Right now—you like me!" For me, it was as if I were saying to God, "I can't deny the fact that You love me! Right now—You love me!"

God knocked me upside the head and was telling me, loud and clear, "Yes, I can use even somebody like you to carry My message." This became a turning point in my life.

I am still plagued by doubts about my abilities and worth, but those two events went a long way to convincing me that if God could use David and five smooth stones to take down a giant, maybe He really could use one clumsy redhead to battle giants in this world—and even topple my own insecurities.

Of course, I couldn't come away from the second Colorado conference without yet another embarrassing social interaction. This time, I met singing sensation Amy Grant in the green room, and I started babbling. I introduced myself as Torry Martin, and I even had a photo taken with her. I meant to tell Amy that she looked beautiful, but my words came out all wrong.

"You look much thinner in cardboard," I blurted.

Amy gave me a baffled look and an awkward smile. "Thanks," she said before getting pulled away by another admirer.

You look thinner in cardboard? What in the world was I thinking? And what must she have thought?

I never had a chance to explain to Amy that I kept a life-sized cardboard cutout of her in our cabin in Alaska. (Of course, maybe that would have freaked her out even more.) A local Christian store in Anchorage had been tossing out the cardboard cutout—a promotional device for her 1994 *House of Love* album—and it showed Amy dressed in a tuxedo. I begged them to give me the life-sized cut-out because I wanted a woman's presence in our cabin.

Thinner in cardboard? I felt like knocking my head against the nearest wall.

I wished that God would stop me from saying embarrassing things. But I knew that if the Lord put His holy hand over my mouth every time I was not to speak, I'd suffocate. Besides, I was slowly learning that the Toymaker loved me even when I made social blunders.

At the end of *Toy Story 3*, during the emotional final scene when Andy is giving away his box of old toys, he reluctantly passes his most treasured friend, Woody, to a little girl named Bonnie, and he tells her, "The thing that makes him special is he'll never give up on you."

Papa G, the Toymaker, is like that as well. He never gives up on me, and He will never give up on you.

Never.

16
THE FLAVOR OF STUPID

I was hunched over my desk in the cabin writing one early evening, and I was suffering from a bad case of writer's block, which in man-speak means that my attention was on the baseball game rather than putting words to paper. I was trying to come up with a plotline in a story called "Forsaken Bacon" about how the Big Bad Wolf became saved. But the ideas were not flowing.

Suddenly, Sam started barking and charging back and forth.

If I hadn't been listening to the game, maybe I would have realized that his barking was more than a simple desire to go outside for a walk. I would have realized that it was a warning. Oblivious, I got up from my desk, my thoughts jumbled by baseball and bacon, and opened the cabin door to let Sam out.

I spotted the bear immediately.

Not far from the front door, it was going through the trash bag Rob had forgotten to take to work for disposal.

Bear? I thought.

I closed the door and waited a couple of seconds.

Then I opened the door again.

Yep, it's still a bear.

Slamming the door, I immediately moved into panic mode. Our cabin door did not latch shut, and we would often kick the door open whenever we were carrying something in our arms. But this also meant a bear could push open the door! So I scooted the refrigerator in front of the door to keep the bear out. This also made it handy for me to grab my last meal, should anything go awry.

With the fridge in position, I glanced at my watch and saw that it was five thirty p.m., which meant that any time now Rob would be returning from work and walking up the trail. Rob would see the bear and start praying, and the bear would see Rob and think its prayers had been answered.

Leaping into action, I ran to the living room and called Rob on his cell phone to warn him. My fingers were shaking as I dialed, and I shouted into the phone: "Rob, there's a bear right outside the cabin door!"

"Shanghai—please place order."

Unless Rob had suddenly learned to talk in a Chinese accent, I had misdialed and reached the Chinese carryout—although as an emotional eater, an eggroll sounded pretty good at this moment.

Resisting the temptation to order dinner, I hung up and dialed again.

"Rob?"

"Yeah?"

No Chinese accent this time, so I continued. "There's a bear right outside the cabin door!"

"Where's that can of pepper spray I gave you?"

That was an odd question to be asking in the middle of a crisis, I thought. But I answered anyway.

"Yeah, it's in the spice rack. But did you hear what I said? There's a bear outside the cabin door!" I thought I was the one who had problems focusing.

An audible sigh came across the phone, followed by a condescending tone in his next words. "Torry, you're supposed to use the pepper spray on the bear."

Rob was still making no sense. I felt as if he were talking Chinese to me.

"I don't really have time for cooking tips right now. Besides, wouldn't the bear have to be dead before I tried to season it?"

Another audible sigh. That's when Rob finally explained to me the proper use for pepper spray. He said that a few months earlier, not long after he shot the bear in front of our cabin, his friends at work had given him a can of pepper spray in case he had to drive away another bruin. Then, when he got home from work, he gave me the pepper spray and said, "Use this if you ever have to."

And so I did. I had been using the pepper spray to season my homemade chili and tacos and burritos for the longest time. I should have suspected it wasn't a spice because the pepper spray gave my chili a strange, chemical taste when I used too much. I also thought it was pretty odd that the pepper spray came out in a cone-shaped mist, but I figured the nozzle was just broken. I learned to carefully position the nozzle close to the food so the mist wouldn't drift back into my face and cause my eyes to sting.

This wasn't the only time I had accidentally used creative ingredients in my food. In another case, I purchased a lemon-scented furniture polish and a butter-flavored pan spray from Walmart, and they just happened to come in almost identical generic yellow spray cans. So I mistakenly placed the lemon-scented furniture polish in my cupboard and the nonstick pan spray under the sink. That explained why my pancakes tasted so lemony and why our pets kept swarming the furniture and licking it madly. The good news was that by using nonstick spray on the couch, I never stuck to the pleather.

Of course, my penchant for mistakes still doesn't explain why I didn't know what pepper spray was used for. In my defense, I didn't know anything about pepper spray because Los Angeles (where I used to live) had banned it. Pepper spray was also illegal in New York, and these were two places where you'd think it would be most needed. Evidently, carjackers in LA were using the weapon to temporarily blind motorists so they couldn't identify the person stealing their car. In New York, muggers were spraying people and then grabbing their purses and wallets.

So I thought I had a good excuse for not knowing what pepper spray was, but Rob wasn't quite as sympathetic with my ignorance. He said these words—and I quote this exactly because Rob is the type of guy who hates to be misquoted.

"What flavor of stupid are you?"

I paused for a moment. *Stupid comes in flavors?*

"Just put the phone down, spray the bear, and come back and tell me what happened," he said.

"Okay," I said, but inside I'm thinking it was easy for him to sound so logical and reasonable over the phone. He wasn't the one with a great big black bear outside the front door—a bear that was staring at our cabin like it was a McDonalds' drive-through and I was the Happy Meal he wanted to order. Or from my perspective, an Unhappy Meal.

But I obeyed Rob's command. Setting down the phone, I grabbed the pepper spray from the spice rack. Acting swiftly before I had time to think about how much danger I faced, I pushed the refrigerator back, hurled open the front door, raised the can of pepper spray…and sprayed myself directly in the face.

In my panic, I had aimed the nozzle the wrong direction and taken a face full of pepper spray.

"AHHHHHHHHHHHHHHH!"

It felt as if my face were on fire. Or I had dipped my face in a pan of hot oil while bobbing for apple fritters. Pure agony. I stumbled around the kitchen, my hands clamped over my eyes, and I managed to bump into every pot, pan, and cabinet. Blinded, I knocked over a chair and then smacked into an entire dish strainer of glasses and plates, bringing it crashing to the floor. Believe you me, I forgot all about the bear.

I also forgot that Rob was still on the phone, which I had set down. Rob was driving home, and when he heard my screams of pain, he assumed that the bear was in the process of shredding me to ribbons.

So Rob floored the accelerator and raced for home at 90 miles an hour—maybe faster.

Pepper spray also causes an immediate release of the contents of a person's nose, so snot was flowing like a fountain. (Sorry, but that's the only way I can think to describe it.) I used my hand to wipe my nose, and in the process I just spread the oil-based pepper spray all over my face. My eyes also swelled so badly that I could hardly open them with my fingers. Still, I managed to feel around in the freezer blindly and locate ice cubes to put on my eyes. I briefly considered using a carton of ice cream for relief, but I knew it would go straight to my hips, not to my eyes. (I'm an emotional eater, remember?)

Still bumbling around, I desperately tried to catch my breath because when I screamed and opened my mouth, I had swallowed some of the pepper spray, and it was burning. The pepper spray also made my throat go numb, making it difficult to breathe, and I started wheezing and gasping.

Still on the phone, Rob thought he was hearing me take my dying gasps.

I plopped down at the kitchen table, and I was holding the ice to my swollen eyes, still trying to breathe, when I suddenly heard the cabin door swing open and SLAM against the wall.

That's when I remembered—*the bear!*

In my pain and panic, I had completely forgotten all about the bear. It had pushed open the door and was preparing to devour Leg of Torry, heavily seasoned with pepper spray. Then I heard a voice.

"Torry!"

It was a talking bear?

"Are you okay?"

And the bear sounded just like Rob. "Yeah, I guess so," I said.

With my swollen eyes barely able to open, I made out the blurry image of Rob standing a few feet away.

"Well…where's the bear?" he asked.

"I dunno. I guess all my screaming and flailing must have scared it off. Hey, this pepper spray really works on bears, doesn't it? Although if I had designed it, I would have had the nozzle face the other direction."

This story taught me an important lesson, beyond the most obvious one (when you pepper spray a bear, make sure you have the container pointing in the right direction). It taught me about the importance of the Bible in my life.

Okay, I realize that pepper spray and Scripture don't seem linked at first glance, but my encounter with the bear made me think of the Bible as a weapon—a very powerful weapon that God has given us. It's like our divine pepper spray for life, and the directions are pretty simple if we just take the time to open the pages and read them. Unfortunately, many of us keep our Bibles (our pepper spray) on our bookshelf (our spice rack), and we have no idea how to properly use them. As a result, we wind up being blinded by our own blundering ignorance.

So take your Bible off the bookshelf, open it up, and get familiar with the content that God has provided. I guarantee that if you do that, the next time you're under any sort of spiritual attack, you'll save yourself a bear of a time.

17

ON FIRE FOR GOD

By now it probably seems as if Rob is the sane one and I am some kind of crazed sidekick. I'm not going to deny that characterization, but I should point out that Rob is not levelheaded 100 percent of the time. He too sometimes tastes the flavor of stupid.

To back up this claim, let me refer you to the Case of the Burning Trailer.

In Alaska, the big thaw usually doesn't begin until April or May, when the ice breakup occurs and the snow finally melts, uncovering all the stuff in people's yards that had been buried through the long winter. The refrain that echoes across the land is, "Oh, so *that's* where that thing went to!"

The snow melt also uncovers quite a bit of trash, so the City of Anchorage sponsors a free dump day every spring. When this story opens, dump day has arrived—a beautiful afternoon with temperatures reaching a balmy 45 degrees. People everywhere were in their yards collecting trash, and we were no exception. We had plenty of garbage, including a couple of big items. We no longer needed the huge foam-lined shipping container that we had been using all winter as an outdoor refrigerator. Knowing that the bears were hibernating, we had stocked the four-foot-wide, Styrofoam-lined box with food, secure in the knowledge that it would be safe from sleeping bruins.

But it was now May—time to dispose of the foam-lined container in the dump. Our burn barrel was also on its last legs, so we decided to get rid of it as well and obtain a new one. Rob nested the old burn barrel inside the shipping container, and he loaded it all in the back of our open trailer.

"Are you sure you should put the burn barrel in that?" I asked, but Rob just scoffed.

"We haven't used the burn barrel for three days. Stop worrying."

So Rob took off, pulling the trailer of junk, and I followed close behind in the Jeep. It was an idyllic day, and Rob noticed that people seemed particularly friendly as he drove to the dump. As he passed by a subdivision, everybody seemed to be looking up from their yard work and waving at Rob, and he smiled and waved back. Evidently, the spring thaw had also thawed the hearts of every Alaskan he saw.

Suddenly, it dawned on Rob that not everyone was smiling as they waved. When he passed two teenage boys, their mouths were open in horror, and they were pointing at Rob's truck.

That's when Rob finally looked into his side-view mirror and saw that the trailer had become a fireball. Flames shot 30 feet high out of the trailer, and he appeared to be pulling a giant blowtorch on wheels. Although the burn barrel hadn't been used for a few days, it still contained some coals, and evidently they were hot enough to ignite the foam lining of the shipping container. The onrush of air as he drove downhill fed the flames with oxygen, and the fireball grew and grew.

I know, because I was driving right behind Rob, and I had seen it burst into flames. I tried leaning on the horn, but this was my discount Jeep, remember? The horn didn't work, but that didn't stop me from hitting it over and over. I tried speeding up and pulling alongside Rob, but whenever I did, oncoming traffic forced me back into my lane. I was afraid the big ball of flame was going to explode, like something you see in a *Terminator* movie.

When Rob finally spotted the giant fireball in his side-view mirror, he immediately pulled the truck to the side of the road. Fortunately, he kept a fire extinguisher in the truck, so he leaped out and began to douse the flames. He brought it under control, but the charred jumble was still smoldering, and we were afraid it might burst into flame again if he got back on the road. So we decided to douse everything with water from a creek that ran close to the road.

One problem. The only container we had in the back of the trailer was an old gasoline can.

This plastic can was riddled with holes and hadn't been used to carry gasoline for several years, so thankfully it was empty. Otherwise, the trailer might have exploded, just as I had feared. He used the leaky gas can as a water container, and he kept filling it up in the creek and then running up the hill to dump it on the smoldering trash in the back of the trailer. The still-hot materials hissed back at us and smoked.

Rob must have made a strange sight to passersby in cars and trucks. This guy appeared to be emptying his gas can on a smoldering fire.

As I said, I'm not the only nutty one in our cabin.

If this incident doesn't convince you that Rob occasionally tastes the flavor of stupid, let me also refer you to the Strange Case of the Booming Burn Barrel. It seemed that burn barrels had a way of bringing out the crazy in him.

One day, Rob set a gasoline can about ten feet from the burn barrel.

"That can is awfully close to the barrel, don't you think?" I said.

"Stop freaking out. I know what I'm doing."

"But I'm pretty sure that's not safe."

"And I'm pretty sure you need to stop freaking out."

The next morning, Rob was outside burning trash in the barrel, but as he dumped cardboard boxes in the can, they just wouldn't catch fire. There were smoldering coals in the bottom of the barrel (sound familiar?), but evidently they weren't hot enough to ignite the cardboard.

That's when Rob's eyes landed on the gasoline can I had warned him about. The can contained only a little bit of gasoline, so he figured it couldn't hurt to pour it on the smoldering coals and give the fire a little encouragement.

He gave the fire a lot more than a little encouragement.

Rob was pouring out the last little bit of gasoline when he saw a flame jump from the bottom of the burn barrel to the can, which was still in his right hand. It all happened in a flash, before he had a chance to react.

KABLOOM!

Rob told me later that the only thing he remembered thinking was, *Boy, that was stupid.*

The next thing he knew, he was completely on fire.

I was still in bed when I heard the KABLOOM, and I knew immediately what had happened. Dashing outside, I found Rob completely engulfed in flames. I mean *completely* engulfed. The explosion caused the gasoline to splatter his clothing, so his shirt was on fire, and so were his pants. Remembering the old rule, "Stop, drop, and roll," Rob did just that, but the flames would not go out. So he leaped back up and yanked the burning T-shirt over his head and tossed it aside. But this exposed his bare belly to the fire that still shot up from his flaming pants. So the human torch pulled down his pants and tried to kick them off, but he couldn't get them over his work boots.

By the time I reached him, he was sitting on the ground with his pants around his ankles, and he was patting at the flames wildly.

"I'm all right, I'm all right!" he said.

"You don't look all right."

He probably would have been a lot more convincing if he hadn't still been smoldering when he told me he was okay.

Rob finally managed to douse the flames, and as he put it, he wound up with second-degree burns to his body and a third-degree burn to his male ego. The entire right side of his face was red—as if he'd gotten a bad sunburn or stood too close to a nuclear test explosion. He also had second-degree burns on his belly and on his right hand, which had been holding the gas can when it exploded. The can was torn apart, but his hand remained in one piece.

After these two fiery incidents, I have to say that I can relate to the prophets of old. I'm not saying that I'm a prophet in any way, but I did get a sense of what it's like to issue a warning over and over and not be taken seriously. When I warned Rob about the burn barrel in the trailer or the gas can near the barrel, he dismissed me with a roll of his eyes and a wave of his hand.

I wouldn't have been surprised if Isaiah had been similarly dismissed by the Israelites: "Stop freaking out, Izzy!"

The prophets were busy during the period of the divided kingdoms, when Israel split apart from Judah following the death of Solomon. During this time, Elijah, Elisha, Amos, Isaiah, Hosea, and Micah all tried to warn the people of Judah and Israel to stop running after false gods and to turn back to Yahweh, but inevitably the chosen people would say, "Stop being such a worry wart!"

Josiah, a king in Judah from 640 to 609 BC, tried to eliminate all the temples dedicated to the god Molech, but this god and others kept popping up throughout the land, like the smoldering coals in our burn barrel. (Ironically, Molech was the god of fire, and many historians believe that children were sacrificed through fire to this demonic idol.)

Today, we no longer worship a god of fire like Molech or a god of fertility like Baal, but we still have our own twenty-first-century gods. They go by other names: pornography, greed, success at any cost, apathy, and much, much more. So we need to listen for the warnings in our lives—warnings from friends who care enough about us to point to the smoldering coals in our lives that might burst into flame if we're not careful. These people are the "prophets" in our lives.

Prophets are like smoke detectors, which can sense invisible particulates well before you even see smoke or fire. So make sure you have people in your life who aren't afraid to tell you when you're dragging along a barrel full of hot coals that could burst into flame at any moment.

And while you're at it, clean up the spiritual trash in your life because God sponsors a dump day every single day of the year.

18
JUST FILLING IN

Alaska experiences about 5000 earthquakes each year, and 3 of the world's 25 highest-magnitude earthquakes happened on the Last Frontier. Alaska also has an estimated 30,000 grizzlies roaming about, but I think what it probably has more of than any other state is an abundance of eccentric people. Alaska is the natural habitat for the odd and the misfit as herds of quirky folks roam across the state.

As an example, consider the elderly woman I encountered one day while sitting in the Anchorage Fifth Avenue Mall, minding my own business. I'm always on the lookout for colorful characters, and on this day I spotted a rare species.

She was a mall walker, and she was dressed in plumage that would put a peacock to shame. She wore leopard-print spandex pants, and she had a purple fanny pack that displayed a large cross and was bedazzled with glitter. Her purple tennis shoes matched her purple fanny pack, and so did her wispy purple scarf. She looked like a retired Las Vegas showgirl, and she was moving a mile a minute as she power walked through the mall. She had tucked a cassette player into her fanny pack, and her ears were covered with large earmuff-sized headphones. Dangling from beneath her headphones, a pair of three-inch, pink flamingo earrings swayed back and forth as she walked.

As she zipped by me, she didn't pause, didn't even slow down. She pulled a Bible tract from her fanny pack and whipped it in my direction, and the tiny booklet landed right next to me on the bench. Then she kept on going, and I stared down at the tract in wonderment. This was what you call speed witnessing. I picked up the Bible tract and started to read it, but I was actually more fascinated by the woman. I watched her race through the mall, flinging out tracts like a revved-up Johnny Appleseed who had ingested too much caffeine.

The lady made a full lap of the mall, and as she came racing toward me once again, she called out, "Did you read it?"

"Yes, but I'm already a Christian," I told her, holding out the tract.

Without missing a step, she plucked the tract from my hands and shouted, "Then pray for my corns because they're killing me!"

Inspired by this interaction, I wound up creating a character called Granny Glockenspiel, mall missionary, who showed up in several of my comedy sketches. But she was only one example of the odd characters that populate this state. Alaska has a way of attracting the fringe elements from the Lower 48—people like me. In fact, I noticed that Alaska was about the only place where I didn't experience debilitating social anxiety, and I believe it is because so many people who come to the state are like me—they don't fit in elsewhere. What's more, because Alaska is still a relatively new state, many residents have arrived here from somewhere else. So I didn't feel like an outsider because almost everyone started as an outsider. From the moment I landed, I felt at ease with the hippies, misfits, and weirdoes. I felt like saying, "My people! I'm home!"

I also noticed that Alaska has a pretty small population of older folks like Granny Glockenspiel. We're pretty much the reverse of Florida. Florida attracts senior citizens like a Pied Piper in sandals and sunglasses, while oldsters in Alaska are an endangered species.

But the ones who remain are tough old sorts—and eccentric, like Granny Glockenspiel and our neighbor, Pauline.

Pauline was our closest neighbor, but that didn't mean she was just down the road. She lived about a mile away. I first met Pauline when I was taking Sam out for his morning walk and suddenly heard heated shouting coming from directly ahead. I spotted a huge snowplow, which had been clearing away the main road on which I was walking, so I hurried forward to investigate the commotion.

But here's the strange part. A little old lady—I would guess she was in her midseventies—had climbed up into the cab of the snowplow, and she was screaming at the driver like a banshee. She wore a thick, flannel coat, rubber boots, and an earmuff hat. And the language she was using! It was full-on Alaskan swearing, which is colorful in its imagery to say the least. This elderly woman would have made a trucker blush. She was perched up on the cab, gripping a handrail and spouting words hot enough to melt a glacier. In fact, the man probably wouldn't have even needed a plow to clear the road if he had Pauline. He could have just put her on the front of his snowplow, and her salty words would have melted every bit of snow on the road.

When Pauline had calmed down and the snowplow moved on, I introduced myself and had a chance to talk with her.

"I just finished shoveling out my driveway when that snowplow came by and pushed all the snow back on it!" she explained.

"Well, I'd be glad to clear your snow," I said, and with those words we became fast friends. In fact, Pauline became one of the first friends I met after moving to our cabin.

I went to Pauline's place every week, and she treated to me to hot chocolate and some of the finest cookies I've ever tasted. Either she had a severe case of dyslexia or she couldn't read or write, because she always asked me to read to her from the Bible, the newspaper, and even letters from her sister. She especially liked my Bible reading because I wouldn't just drone on in a boring monotone. I practiced my acting as I read, bringing those amazing stories to life.

I spent many days at Pauline's house, reading Scripture to her and hopefully planting some seeds. She didn't go to church, although she sure knew how to call down fire and brimstone. She continued to feed me cookies, and I continued to savor them.

"I need to get that cookie recipe someday," I told Pauline one afternoon.

"Sure! Let me write it down."

It took a few moments for her words to sink in, but when they did, my eyes lit up. What did she just say? *Let me write it down*?

Pauline could write? If she could write, that meant she could read!

I realized I had been bamboozled. Pauline had put on an act, pretending she needed me to read for her all along. But I refrained from pointing this out because it occurred to me that what she really wanted was someone to keep her company. It can get lonely in Alaska for older folks, who have less mobility and ability to cope with the snow. So she faked illiteracy to get me to visit her regularly.

It's easy for older folks to be overlooked in any state, cold or warm, but I have found seniors to be deep wells of memory, and they have amazing stories to tell—such as Pauline's story of how she survived the Great Alaskan Earthquake of 1964, which struck at 5:36 p.m. on Good Friday. The magnitude 9.2 earthquake was the third-most powerful earthquake ever recorded.

I also unearthed a wealth of wonderful stories from the elderly people at a senior citizen dance that I crashed. Rob was off to Barrow, Alaska, for two weeks, and I was bored in the cabin all by myself, so out of desperation for human contact I decided to attend a senior citizen dance at the fire hall not too far from our cabin. (The Walmart greeter was probably tired of me, and I needed to widen my social circle.) Although decades younger than anyone at the dance, I decided it would help me observe the mannerisms of older folks. As a writer, I always try to study the behavior of various kinds of people, so this would help me as I wrote about my new character, Granny Glockenspiel.

I had a delightful time, although I was amazed that in so many ways the elderly women at the dance hadn't changed since high school. The gossip flowed as freely as the punch.

"Oh, she didn't make that herself!"

"Obviously store bought."

"She's dancing with Frank!"

"Frank is supposed to be dancing with Doris."

"Oooooooh, Doris is going to be maaaad."

When they found out I was a writer, the seniors flocked to me and began regaling me with their stories. They plied me with cookies and mini-sandwiches just to get me to listen. But I didn't need the bribes because they had some wonderful tales.

Finally, one of the women decided I needed to be rescued from their clutches, so she asked me to dance.

"Sure!" I said.

The picture of us dancing had to be hilarious. This woman couldn't have been taller than five feet, and there I was, a huge guy in Carhartt overalls and big work boots. It was like Goliath dancing with a Hobbit.

As we danced slowly, bobbing back and forth from foot to foot, she'd look up at me and say, "Watch your feet, big boy, watch your feet."

Then she began to tell me her story. She and her husband had both been born in Alaska, and he had worked as a miner before switching over to the Alaskan pipeline. On Saturday nights, they would always go out dancing. She said she missed her husband, who had passed away eight years earlier, but they were both Christians, so she knew she would see him again someday.

"I bet the first thing you'll do when you get to heaven is dance with your husband, huh?"

She stared up at me and smiled. "Oh no, honey. The first thing I'll do when I get to heaven is dance with Jesus."

Then she added the line I'll never forget. "Right now you're just filling in."

Those words stopped me for a moment, and I was stunned.

I was just filling in for Jesus. By dancing with this woman, I was being Jesus to her. But someday, she was going to dance with the Master, and He was going to twirl her around that room like Fred Astaire and Ginger Rogers. I was just her practice partner until that glorious day.

During our time here on earth, that's what each of us is called to do. We're called to fill in for Jesus, doing the little things that bring light into people's lives. That might include shoveling snow or reading for an old woman who needs company so badly that she leads you to believe she can't read. It might be praying for an elderly mall-walker whose corns are bothering her something fierce. Or it might be something as simple as dancing a waltz.

By this time, the elderly woman with whom I danced has probably waltzed her way into eternity. She has probably had that dance with Jesus and many more with her husband.

But I was honored to have filled in. It's what I was created to do. It's what we are all created to do.

19
YIP-YIP, BLUB-BLUB

Sam loves the water, and swimming comes naturally to him, but he could still use some work on his backstroke. He also has a ways to go if he ever wants to become a swimming coach, as I discovered one day at his favorite lake in Anchorage.

Sam went with me everywhere, and I loved to take him to Lake Hood. (Lake Hood is near the Anchorage airport and is the busiest seaplane base in the world.) One day when we arrived there, Sam hopped eagerly out of the Jeep and dashed right past an old guy walking a small, black dog with a harness and leash. Sam stopped at the lake's edge and, impatient for action, turned to stare at his slowpoke owner.

The old man watched as I hurled a tennis ball as far into the lake as I could manage and Sam dove into the water. He swam out to the ball, clamped his jaws around it, and came paddling around swiftly. When he reached shore, he tossed the ball back to me. That's right—he had learned how to hurl the ball out of his jaws and into my hands.

"I can't even get my dog to get his feet wet," the old man said sadly, looking down at his little dog. "Watch this."

The man proceeded to lift up his little dog in the harness by the leash and dip him into the water, like dipping a tea bag in hot water. The poor dog wasn't having any of it. I had never seen a dog able to spread out all four legs as wide as possible so they wouldn't make contact with the surface of the lake until the last possible moment. But the inevitable happened, and the dog went under, although he kept his little head barely above water, his eyes bulging in terror. Then he came rocketing out of the water, determined to keep his paws on shore.

"What kind of dog is he?" I asked.

"Scottish Terrier," the man said. "His name is Braveheart."

I didn't respond immediately, letting the irony sink in. "Wow, Braveheart is a pretty big name for a dog that weighs 12 pounds and is afraid of water, don't you think?"

"He's not afraid of water. He just ain't used to it, that's all." Braveheart yipped and yipped as the old man dropped him in for a second dunk. "Oh, stop being such a sissy. That water ain't gonna hurt ya!"

I couldn't help but feel sorry for Braveheart and his public display of doggie humiliation. I imagined this gentleman and his dog as guests on the Jerry Springer program. "Today's show! Small dogs, dysfunctional owners!" The show would probably end with Braveheart throwing a chair at his master.

"If I could toss the ball a few times to your dog, maybe Braveheart would watch and get the idea. Do you mind?" the old man said.

"Not at all. Go right ahead."

So the old man took the tennis ball and chucked it far out in the water. I had never seen an old guy throw a ball such a great distance. It soared twice as far as I could throw.

"Nice arm," I said.

"Thanks. Used to play baseball a lot when I was growing up. I play with my grandkids all the time. They're getting older now, but they still can't get a hit off me."

"How old are they?"

"One's six and the other's eight."

"If you're throwing balls at them like that, it's easy to see why."

The old man didn't crack a smile. "If ya want them to learn, ya gotta be firm. Just like training a dog."

He then lifted Braveheart by his leash and dipped him in the water once again. Yip-yip, blub-blub!

"Yep, I taught my grandkids how to swim last summer."

"I'll bet you've gone through a lot of leashes," I joked.

"Oh, you'd be surprised. You'd be surprised."

Braveheart came out of the water looking like a drowned rat, and he shook himself off as Sam approached the shore, ball in mouth.

"Can I toss the ball for him again?" the man asked.

"Sure. Hey, would you mind watching Sam for a minute while I run for my Jeep and get my camera? I'd like to get some pictures of him before we leave."

"Not a problem."

My Jeep was a good distance from the lake, up a steep hill to the parking lot. So I trudged up the slope, still feeling sorry for Braveheart. After rummaging around in the Jeep, I found the camera and was just closing the door when I heard a sudden ruckus. The old man down by the lake was screaming his head off.

"Sam!" the old man shouted. "Sam! Braveheaaaaaaaaaaart!"

Assuming the two dogs had gotten into a fight, I came running down the hill as fast as I could move. Too fast, evidently. I tripped, and suddenly I found myself on the ground, rolling end over end like a redheaded boulder. I couldn't use my hands to stop myself because I had the camera to protect, so I could do nothing but let the momentum take me over bumps and branches. When I finally reached the bottom of the hill, I scrambled to my feet, a little dizzy and banged up, and started looking around for the dogs.

They were nowhere to be seen. All I could see was the old man standing by the lake, still yelling.

"Where's Sam?" I said, rushing up to him.

"Out there!" He pointed to the water.

I looked out on the lake and was relieved to see Sam merrily paddling away. But what about Braveheart? He was still missing. Upon looking more closely, I finally noticed a small, blackish thing bobbing up and down in the water right behind Sam.

"What's he dragging?"

The old man shouted his response. "Braveheaaaaaaaaart!"

"What?"

"He's dragging Braveheart!"

In his eagerness to teach Braveheart how to swim, this guy had decided to tie Braveheart's leash to Sam's collar and throw the ball out as far as possible. There was no stopping Sam once the ball was thrown, and there was no rescuing Braveheart. We were helpless to do anything but watch as Sam dragged Braveheart in his wake.

I could see the little black terrier surface every once in a while just behind Sam, and then he'd yip twice before being submerged completely underwater again. It reminded me of the time I was waterskiing and lost my skis but continued to hold on to the rope. The boat's driver couldn't hear me yelling for him to stop. In this situation, however, *everyone* on the lake could probably hear Braveheart.

YIP-YIP, BLUB-BLUB! YIP-YIP, BLUB-BLUB!

I was torn—should I drop to my knees and earnestly pray for Braveheart, or should I snap the funniest imaginable picture? I confess that I opted for a funny photo.

Meanwhile, Braveheart yip-yipped and blub-blubbed as Sam paddled his way toward shore. Unfortunately, the old man had also started yipping—at me! The crazy guy started blaming Sam and me for his poor dog's involuntary baptism. Finally, Sam reached shore, bounded out of the water, and happily ran toward me, still oblivious to Braveheart as he dragged the little dog across the dirt. Sam reached my feet and joyfully tossed the ball up to me, ready for another throw. I swear he was grinning as he did it.

Sam seemed to be saying, "C'mon, Dad! Throw it again! That was fun, but you wouldn't believe the undertow out there!"

The man, still in a panic, busily untied Braveheart's leash and checked his dog for injuries. If Braveheart needed mouth-to-mouth, I sure hoped he was going to handle the duty because I wasn't about to inhale a mouthful of dog breath.

The good news was that Braveheart was fine except for being scared out of his fur and covered in dirt. But his owner was not fine. He was furious.

"You and your dog almost drowned him!"

"How is any of that our fault?"

"You should have trained Sam to come right back when I called him. Stupid dog!"

"Hey, it's not like he was the one who tied Braveheart to his collar."

But there was no reasoning with the man. He crouched down and cradled his poor, frazzled pooch. "Braveheart always comes right back when he's called, don't you, boy? That's because he's a smart dog!"

"If he's that smart, he should have mastered swimming before he tried waterskiing."

The old man failed to appreciate the humor. He scooped up Braveheart and carried him up the hill, trying to comfort him all the way to the parking lot. "Come on, Braveheart, let's go home and get something to eat. You're a good boy, and you know what we're gonna do after we get a yum-yum, Braveheart? We're gonna take a bath and get all that dirt off you so you're all clean! Yes, we are!"

Poor Braveheart. As soon as he heard the word "bath," he looked back at Sam and me with eyes that pleaded, "Help me, please!"

I felt sorry for Braveheart because I had been in his place before. Before I attended Pastor Aiken's King's Way Church, I went to a congregation that paired me with a mentor who really didn't understand how to work with young Christians like me. My mentor was a former military officer, and he carried his drill sergeant personality into our weekly discipleship sessions over coffee. He tolerated no nonsense, and because you have read this book this far, you know I'm about 90 percent nonsense. But even worse, I still hadn't quit smoking when I was being mentored, and this taskmaster had no patience with my nasty habit. He wanted me to make an instant transformation, kind of like the old man who wanted Braveheart to learn to swim and learn it NOW. If my mentor could have tied a leash around me and dragged me through a lake whenever I dared to light up a cigarette, he probably would have done so.

I eventually did give up smoking, but it wasn't immediate. Sanctification is a process, and it takes time, no butts about it. But before I gave up smoking, I was always amazed that whenever I talked about Jesus to nonbelievers at the campgrounds, they never seemed to see the cigarette in my hand—they just saw the light of Christ. But whenever I was around Christians, all they could see was my cigarette.

We need to see people the way Jesus did. He zeroed in on what was most important. He challenged the Pharisees about what was in their hearts because that was far more important than their observance of external rituals. He didn't hesitate to challenge people, but He met them where they were and didn't force them to bend to His will.

As an example, let's return to the story I brought up earlier—the story from Matthew 14 of Jesus and Peter walking on water. To refresh your memory, the disciples were crossing the Sea of Galilee when a windstorm arose. Suddenly, they saw Jesus walking across the water toward them, and Peter called out, "Lord, if it's you, tell me to come to you on the water."

"Come," Jesus said, and so Peter stepped out of the boat and walked toward his Lord. Notice that Peter was not coerced to take this step of faith, and he certainly wasn't tied to a leash and dragged out of that boat. Like any loving parent, Jesus let Peter grow at his own speed. In fact, Peter probably looked a little bit like a young child first learning to walk when he climbed out of that boat and started to wobble his way toward Jesus with tentative steps.

Peter became afraid when he saw the wind, and suddenly he began to sink, but Jesus reached out His hand and rescued Peter, which explains why the Bible never records that Peter uttered the words, "Yip-yip, blub-blub." Like a parent catching a child trying to walk, Jesus was there to catch him when Peter suddenly realized, *I'm walking on water!* and became too afraid to go any farther.

God wants brave hearts, like Peter, but He also wants compassionate hearts. In my experience, the two often go together.

20

AT THE CROSSROADS

Ann Aiken could not explain the feeling, but the moment that she and her husband, Jack, first drove across the Canadian border into Alaska, she sensed that she had come home. It was an odd feeling, she told me, especially for someone who was born and raised in South Carolina—about as removed from the cold winds of the North as you can get.

Ann and Jack came to Alaska in 1982, and they still live there to this day, although Jack recently stepped down from the King's Way pastorate after 27 years. Meeting them was a crucial crossroads in my life, so let me wrap their story in with mine, because Alaska and the Aikens go together in so many ways.

Jack and Ann's church in Eagle River became a way station for transients flowing through Alaska—a kind of Alaskan pipeline for people like me and Rob, and Dean and Larry. Jack says that each year about one-third of their congregation turns over as people take off for the Lower 48 and others arrive. I guess that makes King's Way an appropriate name for our church because the King's Highway was one of the two main roads running through ancient Palestine. Caravans carrying spices and perfumes traveled along this international highway linking Arabia with Syria. Likewise, King's Way became a spiritual route for wanderers who flowed through Alaska in their minivan caravans rather than camel caravans.

Highways have always had a special meaning for Jack and Ann because they first met on a Greyhound bus while traveling across South Carolina from Charleston to Greenville. This was their crossroads experience.

Jack was in his twenties and had just finished his sophomore year of college when he spotted a young woman sitting in an aisle seat toward the front of the bus. It was Ann. When the bus pulled over at a rest stop, Jack walked past Ann and noticed she had a big yearbook on the seat next to her, and the book was emblazoned with a large letter "A."

"Do you go to Auburn University?" he asked her in the snack bar. Auburn was the only university he could think of that began with an "A."

"No, I go to North Greenville Junior College," Ann replied, and she noted that the "A" stood for the yearbook's name, "Aurora." The word "Aurora" would be a nice foreshadowing of the aurora borealis, or northern lights, that they would someday enjoy together in Alaska. God has a way of sprinkling these little hints everywhere along our lives.

After buying something from the snack bar, Jack got back on the bus and noticed that Ann had shifted from the aisle seat to the window seat, leaving an open spot next to her. It was a clear message to Jack, and he says he could "hear that fishing reel zing" as she drew him in.

They talked for the next couple of hours, all the way to Greenville, but Jack didn't ask for her address or telephone number when they parted ways. Ann told her girlfriends back home that she had met a handsome guy on the bus but that she'd never see him again.

She was wrong.

Jack knew that North Greenville Junior College was a small place, so he wrote a letter to Ann and simply addressed it with her name and the name of the college and city—nothing more. The note eventually found its way to her, and they reconnected. Thus began their courtship in 1963, and they married two years later.

Being a military man, Jack's work in the Air Force took them all over, from Wyoming to Virginia to Germany. They came to Alaska because the military had a position for him as commander of a small fuels-procurement office. But they are convinced it was God, not the military, who really brought them there to minister to people like me.

They first crossed the eastern border of Alaska from Canada, not too far from Tok, which cannot even be classified as a city, town, or village. It's a concentration of population called a "census-designated place." There are several ideas where the name Tok came from, but one theory is that it came from the Athabascan Indian name for "peaceful crossing."

It's a fitting name, because Ann felt a peace about crossing into Alaska—the first time she had ever set foot in the state.

It's also fitting that the word "cross" should be in that name because life in Alaska brought many crosses to bear in their lives. Still, they held on to God through it all, and He held on to them. Jack didn't become a minister until he retired from the Air Force in 1987, and Ann says that the very month he stepped in as pastor of King's Way, "We were slammed with everything the devil could throw at us."

To begin with, a 6-foot, 2-inch, 250-pound woman plopped down in Jack's office one morning and announced, "I'm from the church of Satan, and I'm here to waste your time." She followed through on her promise, creating many "interesting situations" for Jack to deal with.

That first month as pastor was also when Ann had to fly with their youngest daughter, Jenny, to an Army hospital in Tacoma, Washington, for major surgery. Three years earlier, Jenny had awakened to tell her parents she could barely see through her right eye. It was as if she were staring down a tunnel because the blood vessels in her eye had begun to hemorrhage.

This was the first serious manifestation of a syndrome she'd had since birth—Wyburn-Mason syndrome. Prior to this, the only sign of the disease was that parts of her face would turn blood red when she exercised. Because of the syndrome, Jenny had too many blood vessels in her face, and many of them had weak walls, leading to the hemorrhaging.

But that was just the beginning. Their oldest daughter, Angie, started showing symptoms of Klippel-Trénaunay-Weber syndrome. Like her sister, Angie had had the syndrome for most of her life, but it didn't cause problems until her early teens. Angie's right leg has an excess of blood vessels, causing it to enlarge. However, a significant portion of her problems resulted from an error during surgery, when the doctor accidentally cut the nerve going to the top of her foot. An orthopedic surgeon repaired the damage, but while her foot was in a cast, the incision broke open and infection wreaked havoc in her leg. Years later, when the incision opened a second time, she was bedridden for five years.

Meanwhile, problems mounted with Jenny. She eventually lost her right eye, and then the excess blood supply began to loosen her teeth. It took doctors an entire year just to figure out how they were going to do the surgery without killing her; it was that complex. The surgeon even took her case to a national convention to get advice on how to proceed because it was a rare operation that had been performed only eight times before. In the surgery, doctors removed a portion of her jaw.

Angie's syndrome strikes about one in a million people, while Jenny's syndrome afflicts one in ten million. Some in the medical community told the Aikens they had never seen a case before of one family being hit by both syndromes.

"When you're going through this, people looking in from the outside can't understand how you do it," Jack says. "But you get up and do what needs to be done that day. It's not anything heroic. We deal with today's problems today, and tomorrow we deal with what comes tomorrow."

"There were times when I didn't think I could cope," Ann says, "but then it was like God would nudge my heart and tell me, 'I will be with you.' He sustained me. It wasn't my will or determination. I knew I could trust God because of who He is and what He says He will do."

As she puts it, her sustenance came from "reading the Scriptures, knowing the ways of God, and knowing His character."

In all, their two daughters underwent more than 60 surgeries between them, many of them requiring flights to the Lower 48 states for complicated operations and long stays. But through it all, Jack and Ann held each other up, and their marriage became stronger. Ann says they usually didn't both get down at the same time; one of them was always encouraging the other to press on. Meanwhile, they took mission trips to Haiti, where health problems are rampant and medical treatment is lacking. They were grateful that Jack's military career gave them access to quality care that would have bankrupted them otherwise.

Ann also says the troubles they faced helped them to put all other problems in perspective.

For instance, after Ann had been gone with one of the daughters for a long and difficult surgery, Jack took her out for a fancy halibut dinner—a welcome break from the stress. But as Ann looked down at the kale on her plate, she suddenly saw a worm poke its head out of the vegetable. "He was kind of waving himself at me," she says.

Jack was about to call over the waiter, but Ann insisted that he do nothing of the kind. In the big scheme of life, a worm in the salad was no big deal, because their life had taught them what is really important and what is not. So Ann pushed aside the worm with her fork and continued eating. Since that meal, Jack and Ann have lived by the slogan, "Don't let the worm of life get to you."

Did I mention that my pastor and his wife are truly remarkable people?

Jack and Ann changed my life, and so did their church, King's Way—a crucial crossroads for me. After all, this was the congregation that had sent me off to the Christian Artists Seminar in the Rockies and started me on my Christian ministry. But now, after several years at King's Way, I found myself at another crossroads. I felt called to bring my ministry to the Lower 48 states, where there was a lot more opportunity.

However, I didn't want to leave Alaska and the Aikens. I loved life in Alaska. I loved my hermit existence in our cabin on a remote 80 acres of land. Why would I even think about returning to the Lower 48?

So I prayed with both Pastor Jack and Larry Wayne, the radio disc jockey who was going through the same process of evaluation, trying to determine whether he was being called to continue his radio ministry somewhere else in the United States. Larry and Dean wound up moving to Oregon to help found a new radio network, taking a huge risk because the network had very little money, and they had next to no experience with such a venture. Still, the network blossomed and became the highly successful Air1.

Dean and Larry left Alaska, and now it was my turn. When I read about a new Christian comedy college starting near Pigeon Forge, Tennessee (Dollywood country), I felt a nudge from God, but I tried to ignore it as best I could. I simply did not want to leave.

I called Martha Bolton, who had once been the only female staff writer for legendary entertainer Bob Hope. She had been one of my judges at Christian Artists, so I asked her if she knew anything about this new comedy college. She said she didn't but would do a little research. She contacted the man who wanted to start the comedy college, and she found out he was looking for someone to direct the school.

When Martha called me back, she announced, "I'm the new director of the comedy college." Evidently, he had offered her the position on the spot during their conversation, which stunned me. Then she added, "The first thing I have to do is choose some students to come down and learn the art of Christian comedy, and I choose you, Torry."

It was becoming more and more difficult to ignore God's nudging.

Pretty soon God's nudge became a kick in the seat of the pants when Rob and I were told we could no longer stay in Cabin Vertigo. The couple who had kindly let us live there free of charge had other plans for the cabin, so we would have to find another place. As if that wasn't enough confirmation from God that it was time to move on, Rob's company offered to transfer him to Knoxville, Tennessee, only 22 miles from the comedy college.

All right, Lord, I get the message. I was comfortable living my hermit's life in an Alaskan cabin, but God wanted to move me out of my comfort zone.

As the words of Jeremiah 6:16 say, "Stand at the crossroads and look; ask for the ancient paths, ask where the good way is, and walk in it, and you will find rest for your souls."

God spoke those words to the people of Judah when the city of Jerusalem was under siege by Babylon. We all go through periods in our lives when we feel under siege. My friends Jack and Ann certainly can attest to that. But during these trying periods, the Lord says, "Stand at the crossroads and look; ask for the ancient paths."

The ancient paths are the roads that have served people well over the years—paths that have been tried and tested and proven to be reliable. In my life, I try my best to stay on the ancient path carved through the wilderness by Jesus.

"Ask where the good way is, and walk in it, and you will find rest for your souls."

Moving to Tennessee certainly did not sound like a restful path. The restful path seemed to be staying in my cabin in Alaska. But the truth is that walking on God's path, where we find rest for our souls, isn't always easy. Oftentimes, God's road is a difficult trail—again, a lesson I learned from Jack and Ann. But following God's highway brings a different kind of rest for our souls. We can rest in the knowledge that we have stayed on the "good way."

So Rob and I sadly said goodbye to Jack and Ann, who had seen so many other people come and go through their church. We also said goodbye to Alaska and its cold, running streams and its eagles, bears, king salmon, northern lights, eccentric people, and moose. I wondered if I might even come to miss the goshawks.

But it was time to go. We had reached a crossroads, and all signs pointed to Tennessee.

21
SAFECRACKERS

When I finally gave in to God and left my beloved Alaska, I didn't expect the drive to Tennessee to be an adventure in its own right.

Rob and I loaded all our belongings into a trailer and hooked it up to a Mitsubishi Montero, which Rob drove. I drove a Ford Ranger—a small pickup truck. My old Jeep was history. When I sold it, I threw in the tow strap for no charge, along with a fair warning: "Don't tie yourself to the steering wheel or to the door—just saying. Also, there are two ice scrapers in the glove government, one with a longer handle. You'll figure it out."

My new car, the Montero, was not as odd as my Jeep, but it still had some weird features, such as an "inclinometer." This dashboard gauge looked a little bit like a carpenter's level, and it told you how much your car tilted to the right or to the left. But did I really need a gauge to tell me when I'm tilting or flipping over? "Oh look, my car is upside down! Good thing I had this inclinometer to tell me that, or I never would have known!"

With my eyes riveted on my inclinometer, we took off on our

grueling journey—seven days of driving, 14 hours per day. My cat, Rusty, stretched out on the dashboard and remained in that position every minute of the trip, so my scenery never seemed to change. It was pretty much "cat in front of mountains" or "cat in front of lakes" or "cat in front of wheat fields" all the way to Tennessee.

We knew we would be passing close to Brookings, South Dakota, so Rob wondered if we should stop in and see Pastor Dan, who lived in the area. He used to be associate pastor alongside Pastor Jack at King's Way in Alaska. But I resisted the idea of visiting because Pastor Dan and I never really clicked. Pastor Dan was the inspiration for my character Sam the Suit for the Savior, and the Hippie for the Holy One was based on me. His world was black and white, and my world was tie-dyed. He was straitlaced, and I preferred Velcro.

Rob and Pastor Dan got along great, and they could talk for hours, while Pastor Dan and I could talk for seconds. On a good day, maybe minutes. Whenever we did talk, Pastor Dan would tilt his head and squint at me as if he were studying a science experiment that had gone terribly wrong.

We just weren't birds of a feather, although we came from the same flock.

So we decided not to visit Pastor Dan (actually, I decided), but we did pull over for gas in a town about 20 miles south of Brookings, where Pastor Dan and his wife, Janelle, now lived.

"Are you sure you don't want to see Pastor Dan?" Rob asked.

"I don't like Pastor Dan."

"Whatever."

After filling up for gas, Rob drove away, expecting me to follow right behind. But when he peered into his rearview mirror, he saw that I wasn't moving. I kept turning the key, and the poor pickup truck's engine would rev and squeal as if several cats were inside the hood clawing and screeching at each other.

Rob soon discovered we had a problem with the one-way bearing in the transmission, a repair that was going to take a few days.

"We really need to stop and get some help," he said. "Like I said, Pastor Dan lives close by."

"I like Pastor Dan!" I chirped. "Let's call Pastor Dan!"

I changed my tune because I knew we were running extremely low on money and needed a place to stay. We were financing the trip on my earnings from the first episode I wrote for *Adventures in Odyssey*, a radio show from Focus on the Family. We had just enough money to buy gas for both vehicles for the trip and to pay the first and last months' rent for the new place in Sevierville, Tennessee.

While we waited for our truck to be fixed, we spent three days with Pastor Dan and Janelle, and I found that I had been totally blind to the man's wonderful qualities. They were the best of hosts, and as we shared our lives over those three days, I discovered just how nice Pastor Dan was—and how wrong about him I had been. In Alaska, I had only known him as a "foyer friend," and it's difficult to get to know someone when your only contact is a few minutes each Sunday in the church lobby. But under the roof of their home, I really got to know Dan, and I think the world of him and Janelle.

I repented of my Judge Mental attitude, but we still had a problem. Our repair was going to be pricey. To save money, Rob pulled the transmission from the truck and worked alongside a mechanic to help with repairs. But even with Rob's assistance, the repair was not going to be cheap.

"We have to do something to pay back Pastor Dan and Janelle for their hospitality," I told Rob as our day of departure neared. "When someone puts you up in their house, you take them out to dinner as a thank-you. That's what fancy people do."

"We're not fancy people," Rob deadpanned. "And we don't have the money to take them out to eat."

"I don't care. We still have to do it."

"Whatever."

As Rob continued to work alongside the mechanic, he happened to ask if the man could recommend a good restaurant in Brookings.

The mechanic suggested the Ram's Pub, although he cautioned that it was one of the most expensive places in town.

Rob stiffened at the thought of parting with any more money, but that's when the mechanic added a crucial bit of information. He said the Ram's Pub was located in what used to be a bank. For the past 27 years, the restaurant had kept an old bank safe against a wall, and they said that the first person to open it would earn themselves a free dinner for four. For 27 years, people had tried in vain to open the safe. For 27 years, it had remained as invincible as Fort Knox.

Rob's eyes lit up.

He was still working for the renowned security firm Mosler, so he knew a bit about safes. Mosler, which is no longer in business, was the company that designed the security system to protect the Declaration of Independence in Philadelphia. If the alarm ever goes off, the Declaration of Independence will suddenly drop through the floor into a safe.

The mention of free food had triggered ideas in Rob's head, and he turned to me and said, "Let's go."

Rob had been working most of the day on the transmission, but he didn't even want to take the time to clean up, so he was covered in grease when we arrived at the Ram's Pub. The people at the restaurant must have thought he was a homeless man straight off the streets—scraggly hair, his face and clothes smeared with gunk. But we were never going to see these people again, so I shrugged and followed him into the restaurant.

"I'm here to look at the safe," he announced, and one of the waitresses gave us a good looking over, probably thinking we were there to pilfer food from the back kitchen. But she agreed to direct us to the safe—a huge five-foot-tall bank vault. Rob looked it over carefully. He had seen this kind of safe before, and he knew it was formidable. It was made of magnesium with doors a foot thick. It would take days just to drill into a safe this strong.

The safe also had two dials, one on top and one on the bottom. It was built with two dials because if one of them didn't work, you always had the other one as a backup. But when Rob tried the upper dial, it would barely turn, and the bottom dial wouldn't turn at all. He stepped back, folded his arms, and studied this challenge. That's when he noticed something curious. The safe had a large round door, and when the door was completely closed, the lettering in gold leaf was supposed to be completely level. But he noticed that the lettering was tilted just a little to one side.

He leaned over to me and whispered, "It's open."

"What?"

"I think this thing is open."

But if the safe was open, then why in the world hadn't someone discovered that in the past 27 years? The answer was quite simple. You needed a handle to open it. The safe had a big square nub projecting from the door. To open it, you simply fit the handle over this nub and gave it a turn. Without the handle, the safe was as good as locked.

"Do you have the handle for this thing?" Rob asked the waitress.

She looked at him in confusion, and then answered no. She had no idea what he was talking about.

"Are there any rules about opening the safe?" he then asked.

"You can't drill it, and you can't use dynamite."

"Well that leaves me out," I said.

"Ignore him. We'll be back," Rob announced, and I trailed him out of the restaurant, unsure what was about to happen.

"We better get cleaned up if we're going to eat here for dinner," he told me. "Tell Pastor Dan and Janelle to meet us at the Ram's Pub and to bring their appetites."

I was afraid he was being a bit overconfident as we returned to Pastor Dan's house, where Rob washed up and grabbed a huge wrench about two feet long. Then we returned to the Ram's Pub, but this time I was too embarrassed to go in. I mean, I could go in before, with Rob looking like a homeless man, because I figured these people would never see us again. But now Rob was going in a *second* time, and he was carrying a wrench so big that Goliath might have used it to change the wheels on his Philistine chariot.

I declined to go in and make a fool of myself. I also didn't believe he could just walk in and open a safe that had been locked for 27 years and that hundreds of people had been trying to open. So while Rob went into the restaurant, I headed over to the Hallmark store, which was having a closeout sale. I hoped to add to my superhero figurine collection, and as a result I missed Rob attempting a feat that would have impressed the Man of Steel.

Keeping his wrench unobtrusive, held firmly against his leg, Rob strode confidently to the back dining room of the restaurant, where the safe awaited. He put the wrench on the nub of the door and prayed that this would work. If it didn't, he was going to look like quite the fool.

With all the drama of King Arthur pulling a sword from a stone, he turned the wrench.

CLICK.

The safe door popped open.

It had taken less than a minute to open a door that people had been trying to open for almost three decades. Rob calmly walked to the front of the restaurant and approached the nearest waitress. "It's open."

She looked at him as if he were nuts. "No it's not."

"Yes it is."

"No it's not."

"Yes it is."

She went to the back dining room to check the safe, and a few seconds later she came running out.

"It's open! The safe is open!"

I think opening the safe must have been one of the biggest news stories in Brookings, South Dakota, in the past 20 years. Reporters from the local radio station and newspaper arrived for interviews, and Rob wound up on the front page with a photo of him sitting on top of the safe with the huge wrench across his lap.

When Pastor Dan and Janelle heard what had happened, they were astounded. "Do you have any idea how many people try to open this safe every single week? You are officially a Brookings hero!"

Even the local police force was impressed. Rob was pulled over for making a U-turn later that evening, but when the policeman found out that this crazy Alaskan was the guy who opened the safe, he let Rob off with a warning.

That night we dined in style—steaks all around. We never could have afforded such a feast. We had every appetizer imaginable, ordering from the menu as if it were a shopping list. The last time I passed through Brookings, Rob's photo was still on the back of the menus at the Ram's Pub.

So what was in the safe? Jewels? Bricks of gold? Lots of cash? Valuable stock? A priceless painting?

Nope. Inside that safe were a teller receipt and a small piece of carpet.

That's it.

Which only goes to show...treasure is not always found in the places you expect. For 27 years, people probably thought there were stashes of money inside that invincible vault, much the way people thought there would be riches inside Al Capone's vault when it was opened in the infamous televised spectacle in 1986. All they found in the Capone safe was dirt and a few empty bottles.

But we still managed to find treasure in Brookings, South Dakota, even though we didn't find it in the vault. I discovered that if you really make an effort to get to know a person, you can find priceless riches inside people you never would expect—people like Pastor Dan. Back in Alaska, I had known Pastor Dan only on the surface, but when I put out an effort and got to know him, when I got beyond the surface sport coat, I found him to be a treasured brother in Christ and a great guy. It's a shame it took a broken-down car to learn this.

Deuteronomy 7:6 says, "For you are a people holy to the LORD your God. The LORD your God has chosen you out of all the peoples on the face of the earth to be his people, his treasured possession."

God spoke those words to Israel, a small country filled with the most unlikely saints. On the surface, they were a ragtag bunch of herdsmen, descended from a wandering dreamer named Abraham. But dig beneath the surface, and you find a chosen people from whom the Messiah would come to save the entire world.

Now that's what you call a buried treasure.

Our neighbors, friends, and family members may not always strike us as the most interesting people in the world or the easiest people with which to get along. They may seem like people we couldn't have a long conversation with if our lives depended on it. But dig deep. They might just be waiting to connect, like a safe that sits for 27 years with no one realizing that the door is open all along.

In the King James translation, Exodus 19:5 describes the people of God as a "peculiar treasure." The same applies to the saints in the pews next to you. We are peculiar, that's for certain. But we're also treasures, every one of us.

22

A HAIRY SITUATION

I was horrified. When I looked into the mirror, I spotted a few gray hairs poking out of my red beard. How could this possibly be? I was still a relatively young man when we moved from Alaska to Tennessee. I loved Christmas and I had the Saint Nicholas physique, but it was much too early in my life to be making a transformation into a white-bearded Santa Claus.

Even more horrifying, I realized that the very next day I was scheduled to give my first major speech. The publisher of my first book of comedy sketches was holding a conference in Nashville, and they had asked me to be one of the main speakers. So when I spotted those gray hairs, a little bit of pride started working me over. I already had my weight working against me, so I didn't want my hair working against me as well. When people see a fat man with youthful-looking hair, they think, *He's young. He still has time to lose weight.* But a fat man with gray hair? People think, *That's just sad.* So on a whim, I decided to truck on down to the store and pick up some hair coloring to brush on my beard.

At first, I wasn't able to find any men's hair-coloring products other than brown, black, and sandy blond. The men's products didn't include red, so I had to go to the women's section, where I tried to find the most masculine-looking woman on the front of the box. All I spotted were beautiful women with not even the hint of a bleached mustache, but I did find red hair dye on sale—two boxes wrapped together and sold for the price of one. I love deals, but the cheapness of the product should have served as a warning. I was too desperate to think that through. I may have been showing gray hair, but evidently the wisdom that comes with a gray head was still a long way off.

When I returned home with my product, I didn't bother reading the directions on the box because ADHD does not allow for label reading. I applied the dye to my beard, moustache, and eyebrows, and then I sat back and waited 25 minutes for the magic to happen before washing it all off.

Then I looked into the mirror again. Mirror, mirror on the wall…AAUUUGH!

Who's the most foolish one of all? Me.

I found myself staring back at an orange monster. The dye had turned my beard, moustache, and eyebrows bright orange. Actually, this was beyond bright orange. This was NEON orange, and I'm not exaggerating for comical effect. It was literally neon! I grabbed the box of hair dye and read that the shade I had selected was called Luscious Mango. I was now thoroughly confused. Was my goal to become luscious or to resemble a mango? Is there even such a thing as a luscious mango? Has anyone ever eaten a mango and actually said, "Mmm, that mango was luscious"?

The name was ridiculous—and the resulting color even more so.

I contemplated what I was going to do next. I had to do something because I couldn't make my speech looking like a very large orange traffic cone. That's when I received a call from my friend Ernie at the local video store.

"We've got the movie you wanted, *Ready to Rumble*," he said.

"Oh?"

Ready to Rumble was a new comedy with David Arquette, and I was anxious to see it because the subject was wrestling. When I was a kid, my greatest dream was to someday become a professional wrestler—the kind of guy who climbed on the turnbuckle and threw his entire weight on top of his opponent. I still loved the theatrics of wrestling, and now I wondered, for one wild moment, if I could travel on the circuit as a wrestler known as Luscious Mango.

Ready to Rumble was hard to get because in Tennessee the most checked-out videos either had to do with football, WWF wrestling, or NASCAR. If Jesus had been born in Sevierville, Tennessee, the three wise men would have brought tickets to football, wrestling, and racing events as their gifts.

"Are you listening?" Ernie said. "I can hold the movie for you, but only if you come right now! The manager is off to the bank."

The manager of this video store never let his workers hold a movie for anyone, not even for ten minutes, so this was a rare opportunity—but only if I came immediately. But what about my orange beard? How could I appear in public looking like a biohazard warning sign?

"I'll come right over," I told Ernie. "But when I get there, I'll just honk my horn. Could you bring out the video? I'll pay you in cash from my truck."

"What? Why would you do that?"

"Just do it. I'll explain when I get there."

I hung up the phone and tried to figure out how I was going to hide my neon beard. By this time, I had performed at quite a few places in the Dollywood area, including the Louise Mandrell Theatre and a policeman's benefit at the governor's mansion. I had also popped up in the newspaper here and there, so I didn't want to ruin my image by appearing in public sporting a neon-orange beard. Therefore, I did what any self-respecting pseudocelebrity might do. I rummaged through my Alaskan winter clothes and plucked out a black ski mask that covered my entire face except for the two eyeholes. With the ski mask over my face, I looked kind of like the masked wrestler, Nacho Libre.

Ready to rumble, I hopped into my truck and proceeded to make my way to the video store. It was a hot summer day, about four in the afternoon, and my truck had no air conditioning. In Alaska I drove a Jeep without a heating system, and in Tennessee I drove a truck without air conditioning. Go figure. To keep from getting heatstroke, I rolled down the window, but it was HOT. I was beginning to sweat, and it trickled beneath my mask and into my eyeholes.

I was trying to wipe away the sweat and keep my eyes on the road when I drove right by the Sevierville Police Station. The next thing I knew, I was being followed by a squad car. Apparently, seeing a person driving around while wearing a ski mask on a hot summer afternoon will make policemen very suspicious. The officer followed me into the video store parking lot, where he immediately turned on his flashing lights.

I was scared to death as he got out of the squad car and called to me from a distance.

"Put your hands out the window where I can see them!"

I quickly obeyed, leaning over to stick both of my hands out the driver's side window.

"Now open the door and step out of the car!"

Obediently, I drew my hands back in so I could open the car door.

"I said put your hands out the window!"

Instantly, my hands were back out the window.

"Now open the car door!"

Was he kidding me? I paused for a second, afraid to draw my hands back inside the car. But I obeyed, this time drawing back only one hand so I could open the door.

"Keep your hands out the window!"

"I have to use my hand to open the car door!" I shouted.

"Okay, but move slowly."

Great! I've only lived in Sevierville for three months, and I'm being arrested by Barney Fife!

Nervously, I opened the door and stepped out of the car, my hands clearly visible. By this time, my buddy Ernie had emerged from the video store, holding a copy of *Ready to Rumble*, and he was shocked to see me standing next to a police car in a ski mask.

The officer looked at me quizzically. "What seems to be the problem?"

To which I calmly responded by slowly lifting my mask, gesturing to my beard, and saying the only two words I could come up with: "Luscious mango."

The officer looked confounded for a moment and then chuckled. "Hey, aren't you that comedian guy?"

"Yes, and I'm working on some new material."

"What happened to your face?"

"That's the material."

After I explained the whole story, the policeman kindly let me off with a warning and a wisecrack. He seemed highly amused with himself because on his warning ticket he had written, "From now on, I suggest you read all labels before applying anything to your face."

I didn't find this funny at all, but when a policeman tells a joke you're legally obligated to laugh. You never know what they'll write a ticket for, so I gave him a strained laugh through gritted teeth.

"Ha. That's funny."

This policeman obviously remembered me from my performance at the policeman's benefit, so I asked, "Would you do me a favor and not tell any of the other officers about this incident?"

"Oh, I won't tell them. Don't worry about that."

I sighed in relief.

"I'll just show them the video."

He had recorded the entire incident with the video camera mounted to the dashboard of his car. Ernie was doubled over with laughter.

I wish I could say my story ended there and I learned my lesson, but alas, I cannot. When I got home, I insisted that Rob go out and buy me something to remove this neon orange color—and pronto, since my speaking engagement loomed. So Rob came back with something called OOPS, which strips the hair of all color, turning it blond. After removing the orange, I then had to add back a more natural red color, so that's what I did.

If you have been counting, you may realize that by now I had made three chemical treatments to my beard, moustache, and eyebrows in a single day, and my skin was in open rebellion. The new color burned my face, leaving ugly scabs tangled up with my beard. I had no choice but to shave off my beard, although I couldn't run a razor over the tender spots, so I was left with patches of hair and scabs.

I showed up at my first major speaking engagement looking like someone with a serious skin disease or botched facelift. I'm not kidding. If I had lived in Jesus's time, they would have banished me to a leper colony and forced me to carry a bell that I would clang while shouting "Unclean!" whenever I entered a town.

But I had learned that there are a lot more important things to worry about than my appearance, and as soon as my beard grew back, I had the gray hairs to prove it. "Therefore do not worry about tomorrow, for tomorrow will worry about itself," says Matthew 6:34. "Each day has enough trouble of its own."

I also learned something that helped me in my comedy career and in my day-to-day life. I learned to share the real me, scabs and all. When I stepped in front of that audience the next day, I told them the whole crazy tale, and they loved it. In fact, after my talk, all kinds of people wanted to have their picture taken next to Torry the Leper. I wouldn't have minded, but my skin had become so sensitive that it was painful to smile.

I learned that as a comedian, I should write from a point of emotional truth. I was honest about my flaws, and the audience connected with me because we have all been there, done that. Well, okay, most people haven't been stopped by police for driving through town with a ski mask on a summer day to conceal their neon-orange hair. But you get the idea.

When the Learning Channel found out about the story, they asked me to play myself in a dramatic re-creation for their program *Share the Shame*, which recounted life's most embarrassing moments. For the show, I dyed my beard neon orange once again, using the same product with the same results.

The title *Share the Shame* sums it all up. We shouldn't be ashamed of our shortcomings. When we spend so much time trying to conceal our flaws, we distance ourselves from other people. I'm not saying there is no room for privacy. It's just that many of us are willing to show only our strong qualities, and we never admit our failings—although our true self inevitably shows through despite our best efforts. Oftentimes, we even lie to ourselves, afraid to admit our flaws.

Paul writes in Colossians 3:9-10, "Do not lie to each other, since you have taken off your old self with its practices and have put on the new self, which is being renewed in knowledge in the image of its Creator."

Letting God peel off your old self and put on the new self can be painful, and it might even leave a few scabs. It can be a hair-raising experience. But resurrections have a way of raising a person's hair, not to mention their entire body.

23
BLACK SANTA

Let me say this right up front. Tennessee and Alaska are vastly different places, especially when it snows.

If there is even a half inch of snow in Tennessee, people shut their businesses, close down schools, rewrite their wills, notify their next of kin, and rush to the grocery store to buy bread and milk. A chance of flurries? Buy bread and milk. A strong wind? Bread and milk.

Okay, I exaggerate, but the difference is still stark. Alaska can get three feet of snow in one day, and a parent will say, "You're still going to school, young man! And on the way home, pick up a Starbucks and Twinkie for me."

But the reaction to snow isn't the only difference I found between the two states when we moved to Sevierville. I think there must be more cars in this region of Tennessee than in the entire state of Alaska. Of course, there's a good reason for that. We were in the Dollywood area, where it was tourist season every day! Cars were everywhere, either going to Dollywood or heading off to buy bread and milk.

When tourist traffic was heavy, it could take 45 minutes just to drive two miles to the nearest Walmart.

As a great lover of Christmas, however, I enjoyed one major tradition in the Pigeon Forge–Sevierville–Gatlinburg area—Christmas decorations. People flocked from all over just to see the magnificent Christmas lights in our area. On the street where we lived in Sevierville, every house was lit up and decorated—except ours. We hadn't brought any decorations with us from Alaska because we didn't have any reason to put up lights on our remote cabin. Why would we? The only traffic past our cabin were moose and bears, and they have absolutely no appreciation for lights and Santa figurines unless you accompany them with festive garlands of carrots for the moose and lighted strings of raw meat for the bears.

But we were in Dollywood country now, so I decided we needed to do something about our lightless house. I drove to the store, fighting traffic all the way, and after picking up some bread and milk, I began searching for a Christmas bargain. I was surprised to stumble across an end cap at the checkout lane that displayed three-foot-tall illuminated plastic Santas—as if Santa were just another impulse purchase. *Let' see...I need a miniature flashlight, some Pez, a Kit-Kat, a nail file...oh yeah, and one of those three-foot illuminated plastic Santas.*

But the Santa I was most drawn to was no ordinary three-foot illuminated Santa. This Santa was black.

There were five white Santas and only one black Santa, and they stood right next to each other on the shelf. But I noticed the strangest thing. The Santas were identical in every way except for skin color, and yet the black Santa was seven dollars cheaper than the white ones. *Hmm.*

I love bargains, so I brought black Santa home with me and proudly set him up in our front yard. But as soon as we set up Santa, our next-door neighbor, whom I'll call Clem, decided to pay us a "friendly" visit. Now, you've got to realize that this neighbor, a white man originally from Mississippi, had barely spoken to us since the day we moved in. But as soon as he saw our Santa, Clem decided it was time to stroll on by.

"You know you have an inappropriate Christmas decoration in your yard," he said.

I was stunned—and not just because he knew a big word like "inappropriate." I was so caught off guard that I couldn't think of anything to say, so I acted as if I hadn't even heard him.

"What?"

"I says ya got an inappropriate Christmas decoration in your yard! Santa isn't black!"

I just stood there staring at him before breaking it to him as gently as I could. "Dude, Santa...isn't...*real*."

Clem didn't take that very well. He told me to remove the offensive black Santa from my yard before someone (meaning him) removed it for me. Evidently, this was the kind of guy who was not referring to snow whenever he sang, "I'm dreaming of a white Christmas..."

So I reacted like any typical Alaskan would when he was being challenged—defiantly. I went back to the store and paid full price for a *white Mrs. Santa*. Then I set up white Mrs. Santa right next to black Santa and plugged her in. Joy to the world! I now had the first interracial couple on the block, lit up in Christmas splendor. Guess who's coming to Christmas dinner?

Not long after this, someone took a pot shot at black Santa and put a BB directly in his eye. I spotted the hole in Santa's plastic eye one morning, and when I shook him, I could hear a BB rolling around his roly-poly, plastic belly. This proved that there's truth to the famous line from the movie *Christmas Story*: "You'll shoot your eye out!"

But I was not about to be intimidated by a BB gun. I simply went out and bought an eye patch and put it on black Santa. I now had the first pirate black Santa interracial Claus family on the block. It was my way of saying, "I double-dog dare you to try that again!"

I was taken aback by the prejudice in my neighbor because I had not seen it in Alaska. In Alaska, we were usually standing in six feet of snow and huddled too closely together trying to stay warm to even care about the color of the skin of the person next to us. Besides, it wouldn't matter because in weather 30 degrees below zero, we all look the same color—blue.

> First Alaskan: "What's your ethnicity?"
> Second Alaskan: "Smurf."
> First Alaskan: "Whaddaya know? Me too!"

Jesus had to deal with a lot of the same nonsense during His earthly ministry. Sandwiched between Judea in the south and Galilee in the north was Samaria, and let's just say that the Jewish folks and Samaritan folks did not get along. That's an understatement. There was an old saying in the Talmud that "a piece of bread given by a Samaritan is more unclean than swine's flesh." There wasn't a much greater insult than being called dirtier than pig's skin.

Samaritans worshipped God and read the Scriptures (although not all the Scriptures the Jewish people read), and they had many of the same beliefs as the Israelites. But they had heathen roots and were therefore considered unclean. The two groups were always at each other about something. For instance, the Samaritans once tossed human bones into the temple just before Passover, making the sanctuary unusable for the celebration. (Some believe this happened the year Jesus was born.)

So how did Jesus approach this deep-seated enmity between Jews and Samaritans? In John 4, He talked with a Samaritan woman at a well, which was doubly scandalous. Not only was He a Jewish teacher talking to a Samaritan, but He was talking to a *woman*! When conversing with the woman at the well, He even dared to say, "A time is coming when you will worship the Father neither on this mountain nor in Jerusalem." This was a bold statement because the Samaritans worshipped God in a temple on Mount Gerizim (the mountain Jesus referred to) while the Jews worshipped in the temple in Jerusalem. But Jesus said He was tearing down this barrier between the groups and added that the true worshippers will worship "in the Spirit and in truth."

Finally, in Luke 10 Jesus says to love our neighbor, and an expert in Jewish Law asks Him, "Who is my neighbor?" Jesus answers by launching into the famous parable of the good Samaritan. In this parable, it is the Samaritan—not the priest or Levite—who is the hero.

A Samaritan!

Jesus had a knack for getting a rise out of the Pharisees and other religious leaders. I have a sneaking suspicion that if Jesus had chosen to decorate his front lawn with a Santa, He would have chosen a Samaritan Santa just to help His Pharisee neighbor see the truth. And if He purchased a Mrs. Santa to go with His Samaritan Santa, He probably would have chosen a Jewish Mrs. Santa.

Of course, He also would have challenged *me* to love my racist neighbor, and that would have been the toughest lesson of all. I flat out didn't care for the dude, but then Jesus never tells us we have to like our neighbor. We just we need to love them.

But before I go any further, maybe I should tell you how we even came to live in the house next to Clem. That too had to do with God's love.

24

ALL YOU NEED IS LOVEJOY

I lay in bed, staring at the ceiling, trying to get some sleep and wondering whether the noise could get any louder. It sounded like a low-flying plane was passing right over our house. No, let me correct that. It sounded like a low-flying plane was landing in the next room.

But I guess this is what happens when you share a 600-square-foot house with a man who was featured twice on *America's Funniest Home Videos* because of his snoring. Joe King, my comedy partner from Alaska, had moved in with Rob and me in Tennessee, but he never told us that his snoring had earned him a spot on national television until he was already raising the roof off our house. If snoring were a superpower, he could knock villains off their feet and send them hurtling backward at high velocity.

The snoring was so bad that Rob and I eventually decided to move both of our beds to the garage. Even then, we could hear the racket, but it was tolerable. Barely.

Despite the nocturnal noise, this small house was an answer to prayer because when we first arrived in Tennessee, we lived briefly with my cousin and needed to find a place to rent. When we found that many of the best rentals were already taken by performers at nearby Dollywood, we did what always came naturally when we were desperate.

We prayed.

"Father God," I said, "if You love us, please let us find a two-bedroom house to rent today, and please—"

"Torry," Rob said, cutting me off in midprayer. "That's not the way you pray. It's never a question of whether God loves us or not. God *always* loves us."

I was irritated. When you pray, especially a prayer of desperation, your words don't always come out theologically perfect. I bristled at the mere fact that Rob had chosen to interrupt my conversation with God to correct me. This wasn't a movie where directors yell, "Cut!" when a scene isn't going well.

"I wasn't talking to you," I said. "Besides, He's a big God, and He can figure it out."

So in an act of defiance, I started my prayer once again. "God, *if You love us*, let us find a house today."

Take that, spiritual mentor! I had my eyes closed, so I couldn't see if Rob scowled at me as I prayed.

As theologically flawed as my prayer might have been, things actually did begin to happen. As soon as our prayers were fired off to heaven, we headed into Sevierville, and Rob accidentally made a wrong turn at the Sevier County Fairgrounds. That wrong turn couldn't have been more right because as Rob wheeled the car around, I spotted a man putting out a yard sign. At first, I thought he might be announcing a garage sale, and I'm always on the hunt for deals, so I shouted to Rob, "Did you see that? Turn around, quick!"

"Why?"

"You just passed a guy putting up a sign of some sort. If it's a garage sale, we can have first dibs. Prime pickings!"

"Whatever," Rob said, turning the car around.

When we arrived at the house, we discovered that the man was putting up a For Rent sign, not a garage sale sign, because he was placing his small, two-bedroom house on the market—just what we were looking for. There was only one large problem—Sam. The man told us no dogs were allowed, but that was before Rob opened the car door and Sam came bounding out.

As the landlord and I talked, he kept glancing over to watch Rob and Sam play fetch. Sam would dash after the tennis ball, clamp it in his teeth, and snap his head to toss the ball back to Rob. Whenever the ball rolled too close to the road, Rob called "Stop" and Sam stopped on a dime.

The landlord looked down on Sam, and our faithful friend stared back up at him, tail wagging crazily and his tongue lolling out of his mouth.

"Okay, he can stay," the landlord said.

I told you there was something about Sam that everyone noticed immediately. Sam had a kind of power over people.

As if finding a rental house the very morning I prayed, "If You love us..." wasn't enough, when I discovered the name of the street where we would be living, I never let Rob hear the end of it. Our new address was on Love Road. Seriously.

"Did you see that, Rob? Love Road. Our house is on Love Road."

"Whatever."

The house was just what we were looking for, although at 600 square feet it was on the small side—especially during the first year because there were three guys packed into the place, along with Sam and Rusty. But Joe moved out after a year in the house because he finally got married after an eight-year engagement, although personally I still think he rushed into it. I wonder to this day if his wife sleeps in their garage.

Not long after Snoreman took his superpowers elsewhere, Rob had a sense from God that we would be moving soon. Rob doesn't always get these nudges, so I take it seriously when it happens, and

I immediately began to pack up our things and store them in the garage. Meanwhile, we also started praying that when we moved, we would find a nice house to buy. Rob said that if either one of us ever got married, we should have a good investment to our names, so we prayed for a house to own, not rent. We even got pretty detailed in our prayers because if I had learned one thing from Pastor Jack, Ann, Dean, and Larry, it's that it's okay to pray for specifics.

We were extremely specific in our prayers, down to a cat door in the garage. In addition, we asked the Lord if we could find a house with a creek, space for a garden, a yard where Sam could run, and enough room to host filmmakers and other entertainers who might come to stay on work trips.

A full year after Rob got his nudging from the Lord, we finally had an opportunity to move from Sevierville. The security company where Rob worked transferred him to Sparta, Tennessee, about an hour and 20 minutes east of Nashville. This only goes to show—have patience. When God gives you a nudge, that doesn't mean things are going to start happening immediately. I had spent the year with a lot of my things packed in boxes in our garage, and if I had to take the frying pan out of that box one more time, I was going to go crazy.

So the house hunting began. "God, if You love us..."

Actually, this time I didn't use that phrase, but God's sense of humor was still at work with the names of the streets we encountered. One of the first houses Rob discovered was on Dismal Hollow Road. He said it was perfect—a fixer-upper, but a good price.

"No way," I said. "I'm not buying a house on a street called Dismal Hollow Road."

"It's just a name," Rob said.

"There's no testimony in a name like Dismal Hollow Road. I can't move from Love Road to Dismal Hollow Road."

"Whatever."

I wondered what the person who came up with that street name was even thinking. Was he in the depths of depression when he named the street? "Well, this road looks pretty dismal to me, and it makes me feel quite hollow inside. Say, why don't we name it Dismal Hollow Road?" It sounded like the kind of place Gollum from *The Lord of the Rings* might call home. But we were looking for a four-bedroom house, not a four-dungeon lair!

Dismal Hollow? No way.

Throughout our search, we worked with a Realtor, and the next house she and Rob came up with was on Judd Cemetery Road.

"Judd Cemetery Road?" I said. "*Cemetery*? Really?"

"It's just a name," Rob said.

I was pretty certain the guy who had named Dismal Hollow Road had also come up with Judd Cemetery Road. This guy must have really been in need of a good therapist.

The next option was on Ash Road, and once again I protested. Granted, Ash Road wasn't as bad as Dismal Hollow Road or Judd Cemetery Road. But ashes still conjured up images of grayness and sorrow. When the Israelites mourned, they often wore sackcloth and covered their heads in ashes. The ashes symbolized desolation and ruin.

"Ash Road?" I said. "No way."

Rob looked at our Realtor, shrugged, and said, "He's got this thing about names."

We were on a tight budget, so our Realtor said we had pretty much gone through all the possibilities in our price range. However, she said that she sometimes teamed up with another Realtor, and he might have some ideas. So she suggested he work with us as well.

"His name is Mike Loveday," she said.

"What did you say?"

"His name is Mike Loveday."

Loveday? Did she just say Loveday?

"That's our guy!" I exclaimed. "I like him!"

Our Realtor gave me a puzzled look. "Do you already know him?"

"No, but I like his name!"

So the Realtor gave him a call, and Mike Loveday said he had only one property in our price range. It was located on...wait for it...*Lovejoy Road.*

"Lovejoy Road?" I said. "That's the house!"

"But we haven't looked at it yet," Rob reminded me.

"It doesn't matter. That's our house."

"You and your names."

So Mike Loveday drove us out to Lovejoy Road, and the first thing we saw when we pulled into the driveway was a small creek running right by the house. Check. When we looked at the garage, we saw that it already had a built-in cat door. What were the odds? Check. It also had a big yard because it was set on three acres, and there was already a garden in place. Check and check. It was a split-level house, 2200 square feet, with four bedrooms—plenty of room for visiting writers and filmmakers. Check.

But it gets even better.

When I headed for the master bedroom, I noticed that the elderly couple who owned the house had placed a sign on the door: Prayer in Progress. Quiet Please. The owners were Christians! Nobody was in the room praying at that moment, of course, so I went into the bedroom and spotted a Bible open on the dresser. The couple had highlighted Psalm 149:5: "Let his faithful people rejoice in this honor and sing for joy on their beds."

I was singing for joy.

Even Rob, who wasn't one to make quick decisions, was instantly smitten by the house.

"What about the house on Ash Road?" I asked.

"Ash Road?" he said. Then he dismissed it with a scoffing sound.

But there remained one big obstacle. Some other people were bidding on the house, and we didn't have a lot of money with which to work. So I asked Mike Loveday if it would be okay if I wrote a letter to the owners.

"It couldn't hurt," he said. "I'd be willing to present the letter to them."

So I wrote the letter and said we were from Alaska and that I was working in Christian ministry. I laid out my vision for the house and how I hoped to use it to bring in people for Bible studies and retreats and working weekends. I even described how I envisioned one of the rooms as my office where I could write episodes for Focus on the Family's *Adventures in Odyssey* radio series. I closed by saying, "It would be an honor to buy your house."

As it turned out, we were outbid for the house.

But the couple decided to sell it to us anyway. "Let his faithful people rejoice in this honor and sing for joy on their beds."

I like to tell people our Realtor, Mike Loveday, helped us move from Love Road to Lovejoy Road. I figure that the next house we buy will be on Lovejoypeace Road, and the house after that will be on Lovejoypeacepatience Road. Eventually, we'll just wind up on Fruit of the Spirit Drive.

If You love us...

Rob was right. It isn't a matter of "if" God loves us. He does love us. But I'm glad that when we pray from the heart, God isn't running an app that checks our prayers for theological soundness. In *Mere Christianity*, C.S. Lewis said that God "wants a child's heart, but a grown-up's head." If our prayers are like the innocent request of a little child, God is happy.

Luke 18:15-17 says that one day, when all kinds of people were "bringing babies to Jesus for him to place his hands on them," the disciples became frustrated. They probably figured Jesus had far more important things to do than deal with little children. But that's when Jesus said those memorable words: "Let the little children come to me, and do not hinder them, for the kingdom of God belongs to such as these. Truly I tell you, anyone who will not receive the kingdom of God like a little child will never enter it."

We need a child's heart and an adult's head. As Jesus says in Matthew 10:16, we are to be "as shrewd as snakes" (the adult mind), but also "as innocent as doves" (the child's heart). Our prayers may not get a passing grade for eloquence, but if you come to God with a little child's heart, the kingdom of God will open up to you.

All you need is a little love—and Lovejoy and Loveday.

25

GUM AND GIDDYUP

I was minding my own business in the checkout lane at Walmart, and standing in line behind me was a mother with her eight-year-old boy. Noticing the items I had placed on the conveyor belt, the lady struck up a conversation.

"You have kids, I take it," she said.

"Nope. Why do you ask?"

The lady gestured at the items that I was purchasing.

"Oh, that! The *Archie Giant Digest* is for my bathroom," I explained.

She nodded her head slowly, gazing at me warily, and then her eyes drifted over to my large box of Bazooka Joe bubblegum.

"You chew a lot of gum," she noted.

I smiled. "Not really. My dad never let us chew gum when I was a kid. Said it made us look sassy. I still don't chew gum. I just get Bazooka Joe's for the comics and jokes. It's a subtle form of rebellion, and the jokes are good."

I motioned toward my six-pack of Cracker Jack and merrily continued. "I'm not crazy about Cracker Jack either. It gets stuck in my teeth, but I'll eat it. Cracker Jack is really all about the prizes. Got a killer skull and crossbones temporary tattoo last week that lasted a couple of days. Pretty cool."

She stared back at me as if I were completely out of my mind. So I shot a glance into her cart and smiled at her son.

"Looks like your mom's getting a lot of vegetables," I said.

The kid looked back at me sadly. "Yeah."

"I'm sorry."

The kid just shrugged.

By this time, the cashier had scanned all of my purchases, and she handed me back two one-dollar bills and some change.

"Thank you, ma'am...but could I get the ones in quarters?" I asked the checkout lady. "I wanna try my luck at the crane machine on the way out. It's got a stuffed Spider-Man this week."

The cashier gave me my quarters, so I grabbed my bag and headed off. I was only a few feet away when I heard the boy comment to his mom.

"I want to be like him when I grow up."

"No you don't," said his mother.

I was a little miffed by the lady's comment, so instead of going to the crane machine I decided to spend two of my quarters on a joke just for them as they made their way out of Walmart. I climbed onto the electric horse ride, which was positioned right by the exit door. I made the most improbable of cowboys, with my long red hair and large body precariously perched on top of the small electric horse. I barely fit in the plastic-molded saddle.

Undeterred, I leaned over, inserted my coins, and off I went. Sort of.

That poor thing tried to lift me up, but it couldn't move. The horse made the most horrifying grinding sound: Errrrrrr-ERRRRRRRR! It strained every gear in its body but wouldn't budge, and I prayed it wouldn't pop any springs—the mechanical version of a hernia.

But by this time, I was committed. There was no backing down now.

Errrrrrr-ERRRRRRRR!

Meanwhile, I spotted the lady and her son coming directly toward me, heading for the exit.

"Have a nice day!" I called out with a wave while the horse continued to groan under my weight.

The lady gave me a forced smile, and her son stared at me oddly. Then he turned to his mom and said, "Maybe I don't."

Clearly, my attempt to increase my cool quotient with the kid had blown up in my face. But his perfect timing with that last line busted me up. As they exited the store, I broke out into a hearty laugh. I must have looked like a maniac.

Fortunately, no one called security.

However, a friend did call Rob at work later in the day. "My wife just saw Torry riding the electric horse at Walmart."

"I'd like to say you're probably mistaken," Rob said, "but unfortunately you're probably not."

Just to confirm what I had done, Rob called me and asked, "Have you ridden any electric horses lately?"

"Uh…yeah. The electric kangaroo was broken."

"You need to be more selective, Torry. People know us around here. And while you're at it, pick up your Tonka truck in the house. I almost tripped on it this morning."

"It's not a Tonka truck. It's a remote-controlled Batmobile."

Rob sighed. "Whatever. The point is that I almost broke my neck tripping on it. Just move it before I get back home."

"I can't move it," I said. "The batteries are dead."

"Then maybe you should PICK IT UP."

"Or maybe you should bring home batteries."

Another sigh.

Despite Rob's misgivings about my behavior, I believe the incident at Walmart was proof that I had come a long way. When I was growing up in Washington State, I was terrified of what people thought about me. I had been teased as a child because of my weight and shyness and lack of athletic prowess, so I was perpetually petrified about doing anything that might draw attention and more bullying. I kept my real self locked away. But God freed me of this fear—to the point that Rob wondered if it might be a good idea if I cared a little bit more about what people thought of me.

When I was a kid, I lived in my own world, where bullies were defeated by superheroes. At recess you could inevitably find me alone on the swing set, acting out the stories in my head. But I never dared to share this secret side of me with anyone else for fear of being labeled even more uncool than I already was—as if that were possible.

It was as if I had a secret identity as a kid, which was only fitting because I was obsessed with superhero comic books. Like other ADHD children, I couldn't focus very well on regular books, and comic books helped me learn to read. I was particularly captivated by Batman and Superman. They guarded their secret identities intensely—or at least Batman did. Superman could have put a little more effort into concealing his real self because he was obviously Clark Kent without glasses, although no one ever seemed to notice.

Today, as a mature Christian, I know that my true identity is in Jesus, and I am no longer afraid to be myself. That's why I am not terrified to march into Walmart and buy Archie comics, Bazooka Joe bubblegum, and Cracker Jack. That's also why I'm not afraid to tell people I decorated my office at home in a Superman and Batman theme, with a little Wonder Woman thrown in to show I don't discriminate. To my shock, the office has even been featured in several magazines and on a TV network, so my secret identity and my secret lair are now far from secret.

I hated myself growing up, but today I am happy to let people into my world. I'm even happy to share who I am through the very public character of Wooton Basset—the goofy mailman I created for Focus on the Family's *Adventures in Odyssey*. Wooton, after all, was based on me.

That calls for some explanation.

While I was writing for *Adventures in Odyssey*, I once met with Paul McCusker, producer of the popular radio program. I told him I was finding it difficult keeping straight all of the personalities and histories behind the myriad of characters on the show.

"Then what about creating a character based on you?" Paul asked.

"What do you mean, based on me?"

"You know, a character who is bumbling, bizarre, gullible, and naive."

Wow! Throughout my entire four years of high school, I never once received a compliment, and Paul had just given me four in a row! The result of that conversation was my creation of Wooton Basset (a name that Paul chose, inspired by a town in England known as Royal Wootton Basset).

The character, Wooton, came from Alaska, and like me he loves to repurpose broken and discarded items. He once converted a car seat into his couch, he made a surfboard into a coffee table, he has a chandelier made of garbage cans, and he has window shades crafted from used parachutes. He exits his house by way of a slide in an upstairs window, and his house is filled with toys that he has been collecting since childhood. In other words, my dream house.

I wouldn't even be surprised if Wooton could someday be found riding an electric horse at Walmart.

Like me, Wooton also loves comic books, and he even wrote and published his own superhero comics. But as I have grown older, I have learned that we are all heroes of a sort with access to powers unparalleled. We all have access to God.

Galatians 3:26-29 reveals our true identity:

> In Christ Jesus you are all children of God through faith, for all of you who were baptized into Christ have clothed yourselves with Christ. There is neither Jew nor Gentile, neither slave nor free, nor is there male and female, for you are all one in Christ Jesus. If you belong to Christ, then you are Abraham's seed, and heirs according to the promise.

We have been clothed in Christ. I like that image because being clothed in Christ is even greater than having a cape or spandex costume. We were created to be like Christ, to put on His qualities of peace, love, joy, and sacrifice, like a superhero putting on a costume. Sure, we all have our own personal kryptonite—our own flaws and sins. But the great truth is that we no longer have to look at ourselves the way the world does.

We need only look at ourselves the way God does. And He thinks we're super.

26
SAYING GOODBYE

Sam was getting on in age.

He had been with us for 12 years, and he had been slowing down dramatically. No longer was he the same dog that could leap into a lake and retrieve a ball while dragging behind a 12-pound terrier.

Sam could no longer even walk down the stairs leading from our deck to the backyard, so Rob made a ten-foot-long ramp that Sam used to get into the yard to do his business. We wondered if maybe a puppy would help to bring a spark of new life into Sam's old bones, so Rob found a little black Labrador at the animal shelter and brought him home. We named him Bear.

Sam and Bear were instant friends. I'll never forget Bear romping around as Sam hobbled along, unable to keep up. Eventually, Sam would lie down, too tuckered out to play, and Bear would nuzzle and try to get him to roughhouse. Sam would lick Bear, but his romping days were over.

Sam had been our protector for 12 years, always warning us about bears and moose near our cabin. I wondered if Sam saw the arrival of

Bear as a passing of the torch to a younger, stronger dog. At last, he could rest from his tireless defense of us and let another dog become our protector. The way the two dogs bonded, Sam certainly seemed to be giving his stamp of approval to Bear.

Perhaps that explains what happened the very next day.

I was scheduled to do a comedy performance in Kansas, and I had my bag packed and was about to head off to the airport. But first I needed to let Sam out into the backyard to go to the bathroom.

"C'mon, Sam," I said, opening the back door to let him out.

He made a few feeble steps in my direction, and then he just collapsed at my feet. I knew immediately that this was no ordinary fall.

"Rob!" I shouted. "It's Sam! Something's wrong!"

By the time Rob came running into the room, I was certain Sam had had a heart attack or stroke. He was conscious, but he acted confused and too weak to get up. He could barely move.

"I'll get him to the vet," Rob said. "You go catch your plane."

"But—"

"I'll take care of this. Sam will be fine. Just pray."

I had no other choice but to go because I had a job to do. However, the idea of leaving Sam at such a moment nearly killed me. So I took off for Kansas, calling regularly to check in on him. The vet confirmed that our dog had had a stroke, but Sam didn't seem to be in any pain. The same couldn't be said for Rob and me. We were in considerable emotional pain, and Rob was about to be in a heap of physical pain on top of that.

While Rob was lugging Sam back into the house and setting him down, Sam shot out his rear legs in an attempt to scramble up to his feet. In the process, he accidentally walloped Rob in his left bicep. At first, Rob thought the thump in the arm had given him a charley horse, but when the pain persisted, he went to the doctor and learned that Sam had detached his bicep from the elbow.

"Did you get kicked by a horse?" the doctor asked.

"No, I got kicked by my dog."

The doctor stared in disbelief, but Rob was not surprised. At 130 pounds, Sam was a horse of a dog.

The doctor was unable to reattach the bicep, and to this day Rob has limited twisting ability with his left arm. The wound is a constant reminder of a much greater wound that was soon to follow.

When I returned home from Kansas, I found that Sam could no longer even go down the ramp without assistance. We had to put him in a blanket and drag him down the ramp, and then we had to hold him up so he could go to the bathroom in the yard.

I was terrified of losing my friend. I'm a single man without children, and Sam was like my child. I got my affection from Sam, and he went everywhere with me—*everywhere*. I still wonder if Rob and I were being selfish, allowing him to linger on, but neither of us could say goodbye. Sam still wasn't in any pain, and we bombarded God with prayers for his healing.

For two weeks Sam lay on the floor of our house, and for two weeks Rob and I took turns lying down with him, talking to him about all our good memories together. I told Sam about the first week we had him and how I stopped at a store to buy some groceries, leaving him in the Jeep with the window open.

"Do you remember that, Sam? I was in the candy aisle, sizing up the selections, when I backed up and nearly fell over something directly behind me. I turned around and there you were. You had leaped out of the window and tracked me down in the store."

Was Sam so smart that he had already figured out that he could find me in the candy aisle?

I also reminded him of the time I let him out of the Jeep and he spotted a big old moose standing on the side of a hill. Fearless, Sam raced directly for the moose, barking in delight. "THERE'S A MOOSE THERE'S A MOOSE THERE'S A MOOSE!"

When the moose spotted the big Labrador sprinting his way,

he lowered his head and shook his antlers. Sam reversed direction on a dime and raced back toward us, still barking. "THAT WAS A MOOSE THAT WAS MOOSE THAT WAS A MOOSE!"

I lay on the floor parallel to Sam, this huge mound of black fur, and I stared into his big watery eyes, which still showed sparks of life.

"Do you remember how Rob and I visited you every day in the shelter the week before we brought you home? I'd sit on the floor and talk to you and give you treats." Eerily, it was a little bit like what I was doing now, lying down on the floor, only this time I was saying goodbye instead of hello.

I told him about how we would go out to the Anchorage mall before it opened, when the parking lot was completely empty, and I would drive the Jeep in great big circles. Sam would run parallel to the vehicle for 20 to 30 minutes straight—and he always remained by the side of the car, in clear view, so I knew he was safe. Where did he get such energy?

During these final weeks, however, that boundless energy was draining away. It happens to all of us, whether we move on four legs or two. Our own mothers and fathers, who once seemed so strong and invincible, become buffeted and broken by the years, like ships enduring the constant pounding of storms. It's the same with old dogs.

Sam was sinking quickly.

Every night, Rob and I talked about whether we should take him to the vet and let a shot of pentobarbital send him off on his final voyage. Every discussion ended in tears.

People might say, "But he's just a dog! Everyone who has dogs has seen their pet pass on."

That's just it. To Rob and me, Sam was more than a dog. I can't think of any other way to put it. Sam was our best friend.

Sam could barely move, but we sensed he was heading for another cliff—just like the time he ran off the cliff and Rob had to risk his own life to carry him back. This time, we could do nothing to keep him from going over the edge and into the void. This time, Rob could not carry him to safety, and neither could I. We were helpless, watching him fall away from us in slow motion. And I wondered... *When Sam passes on, will there be a ledge for him to land on? Will he land in the hands of God? What even happens to dogs and other pets in the afterlife? Will we get to see him again?*

We prayed and prayed, but Sam kept slipping. Then one day he began to bleed internally, and we knew we had to let him go. It wasn't fair to Sam. We had reached the point where letting him linger would be selfish. We had to release the leash, so to speak.

So we made the hardest trip I have ever made in my life. We drove to the vet's place on a cloudy summer afternoon. With Sam's size and inability to move, the vet said it would be better if he came out to the pickup truck, where we had placed Sam in the back, wrapped in his favorite blanket. Rob and I sat next to Sam, our hands on his sides, feeling him breathe in and out, as the vet leaned into the truck and gave him the injection. We cried like children.

The vet was located on a busy street, and cars whooshed by with regularity. People were going about their ordinary days, oblivious to the two guys in the back of a pickup truck, weeping over their dog.

Rob says he could tell the instant that Sam passed. With his hands on Sam's side, he knew the moment Sam left us. And at that very second the skies opened up, and it began to pour down on us. The rain gave us good cover for our weeping.

The vet suggested he bury Sam on his ranch, but we wanted Sam back home with us. So Rob and I buried him in the backyard, wrapped in his favorite blanket—a quilt my mother had made for me.

In the days to come, I was touched by the outpouring of sympathy from our friends. Most people do not send sympathy cards when a person's pet dies, but our friends knew what Sam meant to us. But even more important, people didn't just give us sympathy. They gave us empathy.

Sympathy is when people feel sorry *for* you. Empathy is when people feel sorry *with* you. Empathy is when people stand by your side and feel the pain you're feeling. Maybe not with the same intensity, but they absorb some of the pain, and they carry some of your grief. It's exactly what Jesus did for us on the cross, only He carried *all* of our grief.

Psalm 22:14-15 is a powerful prophecy of Christ's death.

> I am poured out like water, and all my bones are out of joint. My heart has turned to wax; it has melted within me. My mouth is dried up like a potsherd, and my tongue sticks to the roof of my mouth; you lay me in the dust of death.

I can't think of better words to describe how I felt when I lost my best friend. I truly was poured out like water, spilled out on the floor as I lay next to Sam those final two weeks. My heart was a wax candle, burned down to the base. Jesus knew exactly how I felt because He felt the same—a million times more intensely—when He died and took our punishment on the cross.

That is true empathy.

I'm no theologian, and I have no idea what happens to animals after they die. But I take comfort in knowing that Sam lives on as a character in *Adventures in Odyssey* because Wooton Basset adopted a faithful Labrador of the same name. Still, I hope I can see Sam again in paradise. I hope there are crystal-clear lakes as beautiful or even more beautiful than those in Alaska, if that can be imagined. And I hope Jesus will join me in tossing tennis balls far out into the lake, just as He cast nets along the Sea of Galilee. And I hope that together we can watch Sam swim out into deep water and return with the ball in his mouth.

If any dog deserved such a future, it would be Sam.

27
OF MOOSE AND ME

I couldn't believe we were breaking into a trash dump.

Rob had a fishing net in one hand and a can of cat food in the other. I felt like a cat burglar, and in a way I guess we were. We were entering the trash dump to rescue a cat, after all.

Correction: *Rob* was entering the trash dump to rescue a cat. I couldn't possibly have scaled the large fence encircling the dump. Besides, I'd had enough trouble with the police after the ski mask incident. (I had the sense not to wear a ski mask during this rescue effort.) So I watched as Rob climbed over the fence, and I heard his feet hit the ground on the other side.

"Any dogs?" I asked through the fence. The last thing Rob needed was an encounter with a junkyard dog.

"All clear."

So Rob headed for a big, old dumpster in the middle of the White County Dump. We had been at the dump earlier that day and had heard a kitten meowing from beneath the dumpster. The man at the dump told us the kitten had just shown up and nobody could catch it.

The white kitten would wait for people to drop scraps on the ground, and then she would drag the food beneath the dumpster to feast on.

During our earlier visit, Rob had tried to coax the kitten out with the time-tested words, "Here, kitty, kitty." It didn't work, and that's why we had returned at night, equipped with the perfect lure—a can of cat food.

So Rob snagged the kitten with his fishing net, which I suppose made us "fishers of cats" rather than fishers of men, but I think Jesus would have approved. On the other hand, the kitten was not happy. The crazy cat was going wild—spitting, hissing, and clawing at the net. She was so nuts that while I drove home, Rob had to dangle the fishing net and kitten outside the window all the way there.

Because we found this all-white kitten while we were taking our trash to the White County Dump, I suppose we could have named her White Trash, but...well, that just wouldn't be right, would it? So we named her Snow.

Life is a series of deaths and resurrections, losses and gains, pain and joy. In the aftermath of Sam's death, life went on. In fact, life abounded because Snow wasn't our only addition. Our house eventually became filled with three dogs and six cats. At one point, the cats even became too many to count.

I was staying at Dean and Larry's house in California, doing a comedy booking, when Rob called and asked me, "How many cats do we have?"

After counting them all in my head, I said, "Six."

"Guess again."

"Seven?"

"Keep guessing."

"Eight?"

"Keep going."

"Nine? Ten?"

Rob finally stopped me there and explained what had happened. He had been driving along a country road the previous night when he came around the corner and spotted what appeared to be a big squirrel in the middle of the road. Realizing it was a stray cat, he stopped to pick it up, but as he slowly approached the kitten, it suddenly bolted into some nearby bushes. "Here, kitty, kitty," he said, trying to lure out the kitten. Sure enough, the cat came sprinting out of the bushes, but right behind him were three other cats!

We wound up with so many feline friends—strays found on roads and in ditches—that it seemed to be raining cats and cats. I think the word must have gotten around in the Kitty Underground about me. "Fat guy has food."

Our first cat, Rusty, was the only one who had been with us since our Alaska days, and he fell in love with Snow the moment we brought her home. But like Sam, Rusty was getting on in age, and he died of natural causes. A few weeks later his mate Snow died like a bolt out of the blue even though she was young.

Like I said, life is a series of deaths and resurrections.

And then there was Moose.

We had already brought our dog Bear home to live with us on the day before Sam had his stroke. But after Sam died, I always had a sense that we would have two dogs. That had been the original plan back in Alaska before we found Sam.

"I think we're going to have a second dog, and his name is going to be Moose," I told Rob. Bear and Moose would be a nice callback to our Alaska days—although no matter how many dogs we got, I was never going to name one Goshawk.

So Rob agreed. We would go out searching for a second dog to keep Bear company. But I was petrified that we were going to pick the wrong dog. God had blessed us so much with Sam, but what if we're not so blessed this time around? What if we come back with a crazy dog?

So I prayed, "Father, if there is a dog out there You want us to get, let somebody call that dog 'Moose'—somebody other than me." I even wrote this prayer out on a little sticky note and showed it to Rob.

"You want somebody else to say the word 'moose'?" Rob said, shaking his head in disbelief.

"Yes. If somebody else says 'moose,' it will be a sign."

For Rob, this was a sign all right. It was a sign that I had lost my mind. So we went out hunting for dogs, and if no one said the word "moose," I would veto every choice.

"What's wrong with that one?" Rob asked.

I held up my Post-it note, and he just shrugged. "Whatever."

One afternoon, Rob and I made a stop at PetSmart to pick up a toy for Bear, and we came across a big book that listed all kinds of dogs that needed homes. While I went to pick out a dog toy, Rob flipped through the book—a kind of a catalog of dogs, so I suppose that made it a dogalog.

"What do you think of this guy?" he asked, pointing to an open page.

"He's HUGE!"

"Yeah. Wanna go see him?

The dog's name was Billy Bob, and he was a Fila Brasileiro (Brazilian mastiff) and yellow Labrador mix. This looked promising, so we called, and the people providing a temporary home for Billy Bob said to come on out. We drove out into the country, and when we arrived we found two women. One was the owner of the house where Billy Bob was living, and the other was the woman in charge of finding new homes for these dogs.

And then we met Billy Bob.

He had to be the biggest, clumsiest, goofiest dog we had ever seen. He was all legs, running through the house, bumping into everything. He looked as if he were trying to scamper across an ice rink while wearing roller skates. His feet would slip and slide beneath him, and he was large and potentially very destructive. Bringing Billy Bob into our house would be like bringing a very clumsy tornado through our front door.

"Well...what do you think?" asked the dog rescue lady.

Rob and I glanced at each other, and we knew we were thinking the same thing. No way on earth…

"Uh…we'll think about it," I said. They probably knew what that meant.

Rob and I thanked the women, told them to have a nice day, and made a move for the door. That's when the dog rescue lady stopped us.

"I don't know why I'm saying this," she said, "but I feel compelled to tell you guys something."

We looked at her, puzzled. Even Billy Bob stopped stumbling around for a moment.

"I feel compelled to say that whoever gets Billy Bob, this dog is going to be a moose."

Oh, crud. I looked at Rob, and Rob looked back at me and shrugged.

"We'll take him," I said.

Both of the ladies were stunned. "What?"

"Yeah, we'll take him," said Rob.

"What just happened?" asked the dog rescue lady. "What did I just say?"

Digging my hand in my pocket, I pulled out the yellow Post-it note, which I carried around with me. (I still have it today.) The lady read the note, and her jaw dropped.

"Do you always do these kinds of things?" she asked.

"Yeah, I don't like to make mistakes, so I ask God for confirmations."

"He has a thing about names," Rob added.

So we changed Billy Bob's name to Moose and brought him home with us. He's still with us today, and he's still goofy and clumsy and fearful. If a cat even sneezes, he'll jump ten feet in the air. If he were in a cartoon, he'd be plastered on the ceiling most of the time. He won't even come into my office because he's afraid he'll slip and fall on my wood floor. In addition to Moose, we still have Bear, and we also have Willow, a mountain cur I found walking along the road one evening.

Deaths and resurrections. Pain and joy. Lost and found.

That's what our lives are all about. That's what my life has been all about. I was dead when I left California and the party-hard lifestyle in the acting scene of Los Angeles. When I moved to Alaska, I found the total opposite of the glitz and glamor and decadence of Hollywood. I found the polar opposite, you might say.

I found God.

My life wasn't necessarily any easier as a Christian, and Jesus never promises us a smooth road, free of suffering. But handling the ups and downs has certainly been easier with Jesus by my side, sharing my pains and my joys. In Alaska, I found myself chased by goats, swooped by goshawks, terrorized by a mother moose, taunted by fat eagles, and intimidated by bears. In fact, looking back on all my misadventures, I have to say I have a lot in common with our dog Moose. We are both big, clumsy, and supremely goofy.

But I don't mind being goofy as long as I have Jesus.

It all comes back to the story with which I started this tale—the parable of the prodigal son. I am like the prodigal son in almost every way except one. The prodigal son went to a "distant country" to get away from his father and live a wild life. I went to a distant country to get away from my wild life. And there, in Alaska, I found my Father.

We all spend much of our lives running away from our Father. But He's always waiting. He's waiting for us to come to our senses, turn around, and come running back into His arms. He's waiting for us to say, like the prodigal son, "I have sinned against heaven and against you. I am no longer worthy to be called your son." I don't know how many times I said this prayer, because for some of us, walking with God is a continual renewal. But no matter how many times we ask for His forgiveness, He welcomes us home.

While I was still a long way off, my Father in heaven saw me and was filled with compassion for me. In the snow and the cold of the north, He ran to me, threw His arms around me, kissed me, and provided me with the greatest dog a man could ask for.

So let your Father bring out the best robe and put it on you. Let your Father put a ring on your finger and sandals on your feet. Let Him bring the fattened calf and celebrate.

For I was dead and am alive again. I was lost and now am found.

Let the feasting begin.

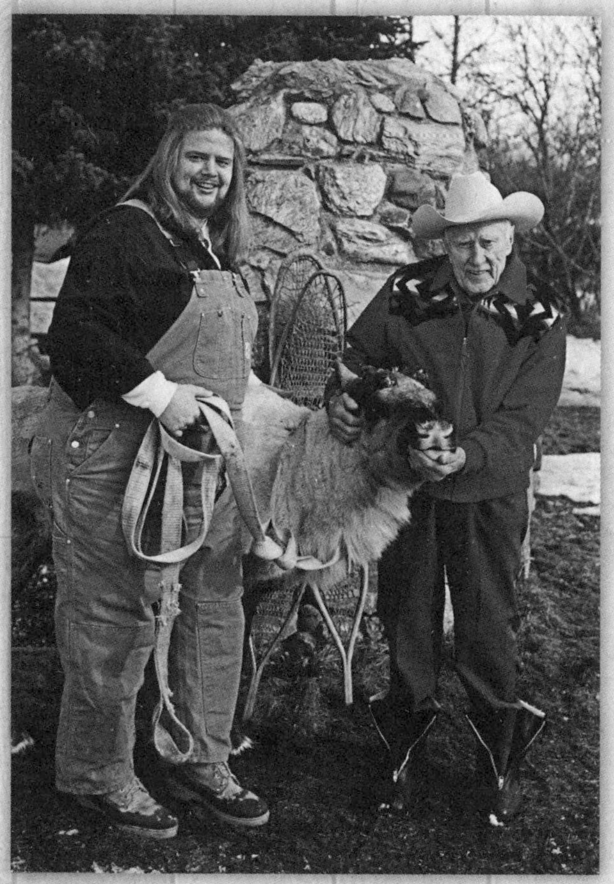

Fashion Plates. I'm sporting my Carhartt overalls, the fashionable Mr. Brewster is rocking the latest cowboy style, and Rudy the Reindeer is modeling a fur coat.

SAM AND THE BEAR. When my cousin Cathy saw this photo, she said, "Oh that's so cute! How did you get the bear to lie down like that?" Sigh. Everything she knows about the outdoors (or wildlife), she obviously learned from watching *Bambi*.

SAFECRACKERS. It took Rob less than a minute to open this safe, which had been locked for 27 years. So why couldn't he fix the lock on our cabin door in *5 years*?